Let's Play GAMES in SPANISH

a collection of games, skits, & teacher aids

Volume Two
for intermediate and advanced students

LORETTA BURKE HUBP

National Textbook Company
NTC a division of *NTC Publishing Group* • Lincolnwood, Illinois USA

1994 Printing

Published by National Textbook Company, a division of NTC Publishing Group.
© 1986, 1980 by NTC Publishing Group, 4255 West Touhy Avenue,
Lincolnwood (Chicago), Illinois 60646-1975 U.S.A.

4 5 6 7 8 9 ML 9 8 7 6 5

FOREWORD

Teachers and students alike know that elementary foreign language classes can be deadly dull. Wouldn't it be nice to break that routine with an interesting, entertaining activity?

Let's Play Games in Spanish was developed for this very reason. In these two volumes is a wealth of games, skits, and songs for the classroom, for parties, and for the Spanish club. Activities range in difficulty, from the simple to those that require a greater knowledge of Spanish. Volume One is intended for younger students, from kindergarten to eighth grade; Volume Two is suitable for the intermediate or advanced student. Games may be played with the entire class or with smaller groups. They may be played once on special occasions, or over and over again. And each one reinforces oral and aural skills while putting students at ease with their new language. The instructions for each activity are in clear, concise English to insure that students understand how to play the game; the activity's dialogue is authentic, idiomatic Spanish.

The songs, games, and activities in Volumes One and Two of *Let's Play Games in Spanish* come from all over the Hispanic world. Educators and leaders of youth groups from Mexico, Puerto Rico, El Salvador, Chile, Costa Rica, Argentina, Uruguay, and Peru have contributed to the collection so that their friends in the United States can enjoy their study of Spanish.

Todo es ronda

Los astros son rondas de niños.
Los astros son rondas de niños
jugando la tierra a mirar.
Los trigos son talles de niñas
jugando a ondular . . . a ondular . . .

Los ríos son rondas de niños
jugando a encontrarse en el mar . . .
Las olas son rondas de niñas
jugando la tierra a abrazar . . .

Gabriela Mistral

TABLE OF CONTENTS

I. CLASSROOM GAMES

II GAMES AND ACTIVITIES FOR THE SPANISH CLUB

III LET'S PLAN A PARTY

IV SONGS

I Classroom games

VOY A SUDAMERICA
(I'm Going to South America)

Any number may play.

Needed: A map of South America.

Each player takes a turn, indicating on the map a South American country, with the words:

Voy a Venezuela.   I'm going to Venezuela.

The second player indicates another country in the same manner. When the map of South America has become familiar to students, the map might indicate the boundaries of countries without naming them. The players take turns, as before, locating a country, but from memory.

As students' Spanish vocabulary grows, the game may be made more challenging by requiring each player to name a product of the country as he points to it, thus:

Voy a Venezuela a comprar petróleo.   I'm going to Venezuela to buy oil.

Voy al Brasil a comprar café.   I'm going to Brazil to buy coffee.

VOY A ESPAÑA Y VOY A LLEVAR . . .
(I'm going to Spain and I'm going to take . . .)

Any number may play.

Two or three of the players in the group know the "secret" in the game, namely, that the word that each player gives must begin with the same letter as his own first name. For example, a player named Dorotea might begin the game by saying:

Voy a España y voy a llevar . . . dulces.   . . . I'm going to take candy.

Leader:

> *Bueno, Dorotea. Puedes ir*   Very well, Dorotea. You may
> *a España. ¿María?*   go to Spain. María?

María:

> *Voy a España y voy a llevar*
> *a . . . mi madre.*   . . . my mother.

Leader:

> *Bueno, María. Puedes ir a*
> *España. ¿Carlos?*

Carlos:

> *Voy a España y voy a llevar*
> *libros.*   . . . books.

Leader:

> *No, Carlos, no puedes ir a*   No, Carlos, you can't go to
> *España. Es imposible.*   Spain. It's impossible.

The game continues until all players have realized what the "secret" is and named a correct word.

UN JUEGO CON EL MAPA

(A game with the map)

Any number may play.

Needed: A map of the world. A list of names of languages in Spanish.

Two students stand before a map of the world while the others in the group observe. The first says:

> *¿Quiere usted indicarme un*   Will you show me a country
> *país de habla española?*   that speaks Spanish
> *(inglesa, italiana,*   (English, Italian,
> *portuguesa,* or some other   Portuguese)?
> adjective of nationality)

The second student indicates a Spanish-speaking country in the world, with this sentence:

Aquí está Venezuela. Se habla español.	Here is Venezuela. Spanish is spoken.

The student must answer his questioner, in each case, with the name of a country where the language mentioned in the question is spoken. If he cannot do so, he sits down and someone else takes his place. If he answers correctly, he asks the next student the question, and the game proceeds in this manner.

CIUDAD, RIO O PAIS

(City, river, or country)

Any number may play.

One of the players is chosen to be "it." He points to one of the group and says:

¿Ciudad, río o país?	City, river, or country?

The player must respond quickly by choosing one of the three categories and then giving the proper name of one of the category, for example:

Ciudad: Madrid.

The player who is "it" asks another one, who might answer:

País: España.

The one who cannot answer within a given time limit takes the questioner's place.

Another group of categories might be *Deportes, animales o libros* (Sports, Animals, or Books), in which case the words given need not all be proper names unless desired.

ADIVINANZA

*Chiquito, chiquito,
pone fin a lo escrito.*

(El punto)	(The period)

TENGO UNA PALABRA
(I have a word)

The whole class may play.

Needed: Individual letters of the Spanish alphabet, cut in small squares and put into a box.

One player takes seven letters from the box and secretly arranges as many as he can of them to spell a Spanish word. Then he mixes up the letters of his word and writes the letters in scrambled order on the blackboard where all can see them. The other players are allowed a fixed time to rearrange them to spell out the correct word. The first person who is able to do this has the next turn, draws seven letters, and the game proceeds as before.

¿QUE VES?
(What do you see?)

Any number may play.

This is a game that is played for speed and fun. One player, the Leader, tells a group that he sees something in the room. The others, each in turn, rapidly try to guess what he sees.

Player 1:
  Lo veo.   I see it.

Player 2:
  ¿Qué ves? ¿Una persona   What do you see? A person
    o una cosa?   or a thing?

Player 1:
  Una cosa.   A thing.

Player 3:
  ¿Con qué letra?   With what letter?

Player 1:
  Con la letra d.   With the letter *d.*

Player 4:	
¿Dibujo?	A picture?
Player 1:	
Dibujo, no.	
Player 5:	
¿Dinero?	Money?
Player 1:	
Dinero, no.	
Player 6:	
¿Diccionario?	Dictionary?
Player 1:	
Diccionario, sí.	

The player who guesses correctly takes the place of the Leader and the game continues. The object of the game is to see how rapidly the questions and answers can be said.

¿QUIENES SABEN NADAR?

(Who knows how to swim?)

Two teams of players are used.

The game is played like a spelldown in two teams. The Leader reads or writes on the blackboard a list of words, one by one, beginning, for example, with *el perro*. The first player on the first team must answer:

El perro sabe nadar.	The dog knows how to swim.
or	
El perro no sabe nadar.	The dog doesn't know how to swim.

If the player fails to answer within a given time, or answers incorrectly, he is out of the game. Then a player on the other team tries to answer. The list consists of the names of living beings, *el perro* (dog), *el gato* (cat), *el pájaro* (bird), *el nene* (baby), *el maestro* (teacher), or even proper names of students, if desired. The Leader should start with words that are more familiar and go on to those less well-known. At the end of the game, the team with the most players left standing is the winner.

SUBIENDO LAS ESCALERAS

(Going up the ladders)

A good blackboard game for about 20 players in two teams.

The players are divided into two teams and each member has a turn writing a word and "climbing" his team's ladder as quickly as possible. The whole group decides on the kind of words to be written, for example, a word containing a certain letter of the alphabet, colors, articles of clothing, etc. The team filling the spaces on the ladder correctly in the shortest time is the winner. When both ladders have been filled in, the group may take turns using the words in sentences. Then another category of words may be chosen for another round. A model of the ladders, in which the words must contain the letter ñ, might look like this:

Escalera 1		Escalera 2
6. soñar		
5. España		5. sueño
4. mañana		4. español
3. niño		3. año
2. baño		2. enseñar
1. señora		1. niña

VAMOS A VIAJAR

(Let's take a trip)

Up to 40 may play the game, in two relay teams.

Needed: Two large maps of Latin America. A pencil. A card or paper for each player on which are written the names of two Latin American cities, such as, *Quito—Panamá, Lima—Caracas.* etc.

Each player in turn goes to his team's map and draws a line connecting his two cities as quickly as he can. He calls out the names as he does so. If he cannot find the cities on the map within a set time, or if he mispronounces the names, he returns to his place, and another takes his place. The team which finishes all its cards first is the winner.

The game may be played in the same manner with large maps of Europe, and the cards have names of cities in Spain paired with cities of other countries of Europe.

LES PRESENTO A UN AMIGO

(I present a friend to you)

12 or 14 players is a good number for this game, in which students practice introducing each other.

Each player chooses a partner. Within three minutes he learns three things about this partner by asking these questions:

¿Cómo se llama usted?	What is your name?
¿De dónde es?	Where are you from?
¿Cuál es su pasatiempo favorito?	What is your favorite pastime?

After the three minutes are over, one player introduces his partner to the group:

Quiero presentarles a mi amigo Tomás Balbuena.

Group:

Mucho gusto. Mucho gusto en conocerle. Tanto gusto.	Glad to meet you, etc.

Tomás:

El gusto es mío. Gracias.	The pleasure is mine. Thank you.

Player 1:

Tomás es de Nueva York.	Tomás is from New York.
Su pasatiempo favorito es viajar.	His favorite pastime is travelling.

The game continues with another player introducing his partner to the group in the same manner.

PALABRAS QUE TERMINAN EN "MENTE"

(Words that end in "ly")

Any number may play.

Players are standing. Each one, in turn, must give a word ending in "mente." If a player repeats one of the words already given or fails to respond within an alloted time, he must sit down. For more advanced students, it might be required that each new adverb begin with the next letter of the alphabet (omitting the letters *k, w,* and *x,* and perhaps *y.*)

The game may also be played with players divided into teams and members of each alternating in giving words. The winning team is the one with more players left standing at the end of a given time.

¿QUE HAY EN LA CIUDAD?

(What is there in the city?)

Any number may play.

Needed: A list of cities of the world on the blackboard.

The Leader calls out the name of one of the cities and one player must use the name of the city in a sentence, together with a noun of occupation that begins with the same initial letter. For example, if the Leader calls out *"Buenos Aires,"*

Player:

En Buenos Aires hay bailadores.	There are dancers in . . .
En Santiago hay sastres.	There are tailors in . . .

Names of countries, states, regions, etc. may be substituted for cities.

Another version may use the names of foods, in the following pattern:

Tengo lechuga en Lima.	I have lettuce in . . .
Tengo uvas en el Uruguay.	I have grapes in . . .

TRABALENGUAS

(Tongue twister)

There is no more challenging test of oral skill than a tongue twister. Here is one:

La feliz emperatriz despierta, reza sus oraciones y empieza a vestirse. La feliz emperatriz tiene cruz de oro. Desayuna con arroz y azúcar.	The happy empress awakens, says her prayers and begins to dress herself. The happy empress has a cross of gold and breakfasts on rice and sugar.

¿DONDE ESTA?

(Where is it?)

Up to 40 may play.

Needed: Any convenient object to be hidden.

One player is sent out of the room and the others decide upon a pencil, a key, etc. to be placed somewhere in the room. One of the players goes to the door and speaks to the person who has been sent out:

Pase usted.	Come in.

Player 1:

Gracias.	Thank you.

As Player 1 comes in, another player asks him:

¿Dónde está el lápiz?	Where is the pencil?
(la llave, etc.)	(the key, etc.)

Player 1:

No sé.	I don't know.

Player 3:

Búsquelo (la).	Look for it.

Player 1 begins a search for the object as the group counts in unison: "*Uno, dos, tres,* etc." They count as far as they wish to go. When Player 1 approaches the hidden article, their voices are raised; when Player 1 goes farther away, the words are spoken softly. When the object has been found, Player 1 holds it up before the class and says:

Aquí está. Aquí está	Here it is. Here's the pencil.
el lápiz.	

(Once a red pencil was hidden in a girl's pony tail and the player never did discover it.)

✿ ✿ ✿ ✿ ✿

Another way to play the game.

While Player 1 is looking for the object, the group says in unison the days of the week, or the months of the year.

✿ ✿ ✿ ✿ ✿

In English-speaking countries, we say in unison: "You're cold" or "You're hot." In some Spanish-speaking countries the players say these words to the seeker:

Frío, frío, frío,   Cold cold, cold,
    como las aguas del río.   like the waters of the river.

When the player approaches the hidden object the players say:

Calor, calor, calor, que se   Heat, heat, heat, that burns,
    quema, que se quema . . .   burns . . .

¿QUE DESAPARECIO?

(What disappeared?)

Any number may play.

Needed: a table on which has been placed a number of small objects such as a book, pencil, notebook, ball, pen, flower, handkerchief, paper, envelope, pin, magazine—objects whose Spanish names are familiar to students.

The group is given a specified time to observe the objects. Then they turn their heads and the leader removes an object from the table.

Leader:
    ¿Qué desapareció?

The first player to guess what is missing takes the Leader's place. The article that was removed is put back, the players turn their heads again, and the new Leader removes another object. The game continues as before.

EL TESORO

(The treasure)

An individual or a group may play this game.

Needed: If desired, on the blackboard a list of countries and the names of their most important resources.

The Leader tells the students that they are treasure hunters and then asks:

¿Adónde va a buscar esmeraldas?	Where do you go to look for emeralds?
Player 1:	
Voy a buscar esmeraldas en Colombia.	I'm going to look for emeralds in Colombia.

If the player cannot answer, another takes a turn. When the question has been answered, the Leader proceeds:

¿Adónde va a buscar oro (diamantes, perlas, plata, etc.)?	. . . gold (diamonds, pearls, silver, etc.)

The Leader may repeat a question he has already asked or form a new one, as players try to respond in turn as quickly and accurately as they can.

ADIVINANZA

(Riddle)

Students enjoy riddles as much in a foreign language as in their own. Here is one:

Mientras me matan, lloran. *¿Qué soy?*	While they kill me, they cry. What am I?
(La cebolla)	(The onion)

¿QUIEN ES?
(Who is it?)

Any number may play.

One player is chosen to go first. He secretly selects another of the group as the "unknown person." Everyone in the group has a turn asking a question until the person's identity is revealed. The dialogue might sound like this:

Questioner 1:
¿Es alto?	Is he tall?

Player 1:
Sí, es alta.	Yes, she is tall.

Questioner 2:
Ah, es muchacha. ¿Lleva una blusa blanca?	Oh, it's a girl. Is she wearing a white blouse?

Player 1:
No, no lleva una blusa blanca.	No, she is not . . .

Questioner 3:
¿Lleva una falda amarilla?	Is she wearing a yellow skirt?

The questioning continues until the person's identity is learned. Then someone else selects another "unknown" and the game proceeds as before.

ADIVINANZA

A pesar de que tengo patas, yo no me puedo mover;	Although I have legs, I can't move myself;
llevo encima la comida y no me la puedo comer.	I carry the meal on top and I can't eat it.
(La mesa)	(The table)

¿DONDE ESTOY?

(Where am I?)

Any number may play.

Needed: If desired, a list of possible locations may be put on the blackboard for less experienced students.

One player is chosen to be "It." He selects for himself a location (city, region, well-known landmark) and the others question him in an effort to learn where he is.

Questioner 1:
  ¿Está Ud. en el Ecuador? Are you in Ecuador?

Player 1:
  No, no estoy en el Ecuador.

Questioner 2:
  ¿Está Ud. en España?

Player 1:
  Sí, estoy en España.

Questioner 3:
  ¿Está Ud. en la playa? Are you on the beach?

Player 1:
  No, no estoy en la playa.

Questioner 4:
  ¿Hace frío? Is it cold?

Player 1:
  No, no hace frío.

Questioner 5:
  ¿Hay flores? Are there flowers?

Player 1:
  Sí, hay flores.

Questioner 6:
   ¿Está Ud. en Sevilla?

Player 1:
   Sí, estoy en Sevilla.

The one who has guessed correctly becomes "It" and the game proceeds as before.

ALGUIEN SE SEMEJA A USTED

(Someone resembles you)

15 to 20 may play.

Someone is chosen to be "It" (*El*). One of the players starts the game by saying to him:

Hay alguien que se semeja a usted.

El: *¿A mí? ¿Cómo?*	Me? In what way?

Player 1 (giving a clue):
   Tiene dos hermanos, como
      Ud.
	He has two brothers, like you.

El: *No sé quién será.*	I don't know who it can be.
Player 2: *Le gusta nadar.*	He likes to swim.
El: *¿Es Julio?*	
Player 2: *No, no es Julio.*	
Player 3: *Vive en una casa blanca.*	He lives in a white house.

El:
   ¿Es Pepita?

Player 3:
   No es Pepita.

The game continues with more clues given by different players, showing other similarities between "It" and the chosen person. If the former is unable to learn the identity of the "Unknown," he can say:

Me doy por vencido.   I give up.

The last player who gave a clue answers then:

Es Tomás.

The one who last gave a clue now becomes "It" and the game continues.

¿CUANDO? ¿POR QUE? ¿DONDE?
(When? Why? Where?)

From 2 to 20 may play.

One player leaves the room and the others select an object which he is to guess. When he returns, he questions the group as follows:

¿Cuándo lo usa?	When do you use it?

#1:

Todos los días y todas las noches.	Every day and every night.

Player:

¿Por qué lo usa?	Why do you use it?

#2:

Para averiguar algo.	To find out something.

Player:

¿En dónde lo usa?	Where do you use it?

#3:

En todas partes: en mi casa, en la escuela, en el centro.	Everywhere: in my house, at school, downtown.

The player continues asking the three questions until he can guess, for example:

¿Es el reloj?	Is it the clock?

#4:

Sí, es el reloj.

Then someone else leaves the room, another object is chosen, and the second player questions the group in the same way as before.

LOS EXPLORADORES

(The explorers)

Any number may play.

Needed: If desired, a list of famous explorers on the blackboard.

One player takes the part of an *explorador* and the others take turns questioning him to find out who he is.

Player 1:

¿Es usted español?	Are you a Spaniard?

Explorador:

Sí, soy español.

Player 2:

¿Es usted explorador de los Estados Unidos?	Are you an explorer of the United States?

Explorador:

No, señorita.

Player 3:
   ¿Es usted explorador de   Are you an explorer of
     la América del Sur?   South America?

Explorador:
   No, señor, en la América
    del Sur, no.

Player 4:
   ¿Es usted explorador de
    México?

Explorador:
   Sí, señorita, en México.

Player 5:
   ¿Es usted Hernán Cortés?

Explorador:
   Sí, soy Hernán Cortés.

A new explorer is chosen and the game continues.

¿PARA QUE SIRVE?

(What purpose does it serve?)

A large-sized group may play this guessing game.

One player begins the game by saying:

   Estoy pensando en algo.   I am thinking of something.

Player 2:
   ¿Piensa usted en una   Are you thinking of a
    persona o una cosa?   person or a thing.

Player 1:
   Pienso en una cosa.   I am thinking of a thing.

Player 3:
   ¿Para qué sirve?   What purpose does it serve?

Player 1:
  Da informes.   It gives information.
Various players:
  ¿Es un libro? ¿Es   Is it a book? Is it a
    una clase? etc.   class? etc.

Player 1:
  No.

Players:
  Nos damos por vencidos.   We give up.

Player 1:
  Es la hora de las noticias en   It's the news hour on
    televisión.   television.

The first player might say:
No sirve para nada.   It's good for nothing.

After several guesses, he might answer something like:

Es mi motocicleta.   It's my motorcycle.
  No sirve. Está   It doesn't run. It's broken.
  descompuesta.

UNA ENSALADA DE FRUTAS, POR FAVOR

(A fruit salad, please)

About 15 players.

Needed: A list of fruits as long as possible.

The Leader takes the part of a waiter, or one of the group may do so. A player of the group says:

Una ensalada de frutas, por favor.

Leader:
  ¿Con qué frutas, señor?   With what fruits, sir?

Player 1:
  Con plátanos y piña.   With bananas and pineapple.

Leader (repeating):
   *Una ensalada de plátanos
      y piña.*

Player 1:
   Gracias.

Another player orders his fruit salad.

Quiero una ensalada de duraznos, fresas, toronja y plátano.	I want a salad of peaches, strawberries, grapefruit, and banana.

The Leader calls on each player in turn as the game continues.

UN SANDWICH, POR FAVOR

(A sandwich, please)

Up to 40 may play.

Needed: If desired, a list on the blackboard of foods that might be used in sandwiches.

Each player in turn "orders" a sandwich in this manner:

Un sandwich, por favor.

Leader:

¿Qué clase de sandwich, señor?	What kind of sandwich, sir?

Player 1:

Un sandwich con rosbif, lechuga y mayonesa.	A sandwich with roast beef, lettuce, and mayonnaise.

Leader: (repeats)

Rosbif, lechuga y mayonesa. Aquí lo tiene usted, señor.	Here you are, sir.

Player 1:
   Gracias.

The next player comes forward and orders his sandwich.

Player 2:
Un sandwich de jamón y mostaza con pan de centeno.	A ham and mustard sandwich on rye.

Leader:
¿Con lechuga?	With lettuce?

Player 2:
No, sin lechuga.	No, without.

The game continues in this way. Students may order what they wish on their sandwiches, even trying for humorous effect with unusual combinations.

EL EXTRANJERO

(The foreigner)

Up to 40 may play, divided into pairs.

One of each couple is a foreigner who has just arrived in the town of San Martín, who will ask of his partner, a native, as many logical questions as he might want answered. Couples are given a short period to plan their dialogues, which they then present in turn before the group. The others may wish to judge which couple have the most spontaneous and interesting conversation. Perhaps some couples will make the conversations humorous. These are some of the questions that may be asked:

¿Puede usted decirme dónde está la botica?	Can you tell me where the drugstore is?
¿A qué hora sale el autobús para Teotihuacán?	What time does the bus leave for Teotihuacan?
Dispense usted, ¿dónde puedo comprar un boleto para San Juan del Lago?	Excuse me, where can I buy a ticket for San Juan del Lago?

¿QUE VOY A NECESITAR EN MI TRABAJO?

(What am I going to need in my work?)

Up to 30 may play.

Needed: If desired, lists of nouns of occupation and tools on the blackboard.

One player leaves the room. The others decide on a profession for him. When he returns he tries to discover his profession by asking other players what he will need.

Player 1:
   ¿Qué voy a necesitar en mi trabajo?

Player 2:
   Usted va a necesitar una sierra.   You're going to need a saw.

Player 1:
   ¿Soy leñador?   Am I a woodcutter?

Player 3:
   No, usted no es leñador.

Player 1:
   ¿Soy carpintero?   Am I a carpenter?

Player 4:
   Sí, usted es carpintero.

Another player then takes a turn.

ADIVINANZA

Lo llevas a tu boca y no lo comes.   You put it to your mouth and you don't eat it.

(*El tenedor* or *la cucharita*)   (The fork or the teaspoon)

VEINTE PREGUNTAS

(Twenty questions)

Any number may play.

This game is played as in English, with players taking turns asking a series of twenty questions of the Leader, in an effort to ascertain the secret word. Each time the Leader answers, he must name a proper noun in the category in question, in the following manner:

Player 1:
   ¿Es una ciudad?   Is it a city?

Leader:
   No, no es Nueva York.   No, it isn't New York.

Player 2:
   ¿Es una película?   Is it a movie?

Leader:
   No, no es "El doctor
      Zhivago."   No, it isn't " Dr. Zhivago."

Player 3:
   ¿Es un país?   Is it a country?

Leader:
   No, no es España.   No, it isn't Spain.

Player 4:
   ¿Es un hombre?   Is it a man?

Leader:
   Sí, pero no es Fidel Castro.   Yes, but it isn't Fidel Castro.

Player 5:
   ¿Es norteamericano?   Is he North American?

Leader:
   No, no es el presidente
      Nixon.   No, it isn't President Nixon.

If the secret word has not been guessed after twenty questions, the Leader reveals it. If a player discovers the secret word, he becomes the Leader for the next round. Otherwise a new Leader is chosen by the students.

LEGUMBRES, MINERALES, ANIMALES

(Vegetable, mineral, or animal)

This is also played like the English version of Twenty Questions. Any number may play.

The Leader has in mind something or someone specific, and players are permitted to ask him, one by one, twenty questions to try to find out what it is.

Player 1:
  ¿Es legumbre, mineral o animal?

Leader:
  Es animal.

Player 2:
  ¿Es hombre?   Is it a man?

Leader:
  No, no es hombre.

Player 3:
  ¿Es un animal salvaje?   Is it a wild animal?

Leader:
  No, no es salvaje.

Player 4:
  ¿Es gato?   Is it a cat?

Leader:
  No, no es gato.

Player 5:
  ¿Es perro?   Is it a dog?

Leader:
  Sí, es perro.

Player 6:
  ¿Es un perro que trabaja   Is it a dog that plays in the
    en el cine?   movies?

Leader:
  No, no trabaja en el cine.

Player 7:
  ¿Es el perro del Presidente?   Is it the President's dog?

Leader:
  Sí, es el perro del Presidente.

COMPARACIONES

(Comparisons)

Spanish-speaking people like to use vigorous comparisons in their language. Students will find it challenging to practice adjective usage by making comparisons of this kind. Any number may play.

Students are divided into two teams. A player on one team calls out an adjective or an adverb, such as *valiente.* A player on the other side must use the word in a comparison, as:

  Tan valiente como un león.   As brave as a lion.
   or
  Más valiente que el Cid.   Braver than the Cid.

If he does so correctly, he calls out the next word and a member of the first team must reply. The teams alternate in this manner, and if a player fails to answer correctly, another member of his own team tries, until a correct comparison has been made.

SOY UN ANIMAL

(I am an animal)

Up to 30 may play.

The player who is "It" decides which animal he will represent and the others try to find out who he is with such questions as the following:

Player 1:
  ¿Tiene cuatro patas?   Have you four feet?

"It":
  Sí, tengo cuatro patas.

Player 2:
  ¿Puede usted caminar
    aprisa?   Can you go fast?

"It":
  No, no camino aprisa.

Player 3:
  ¿Ayuda usted al hombre?   Do you help man?

"It":
  Sí, ayudo al hombre.

The one who guesses correctly becomes the next animal.

TRABALENGUAS

¿Tú techas tu choza   Are you putting a roof on
  o techas la ajena?   your hut, or a roof on
                                    the one next door?

Ni techo mi choza,   I'm not putting a roof on my
  ni techo la ajena,   hut,   nor a roof on the one
  que techo la choza   next door; I'm putting a
  de María Chucena.   roof on the hut of Maria
                                    Chucena.

LOS CONTRASTES

(Contrasts)

Any number may play, divided into two teams. The game provides good practice in using adjectives correctly.

One player of the first team forms a descriptive sentence, in this manner:

Burgos es una ciudad vieja.   Burgos is an old city.

A player on the other side, as quickly as possible, replies with a contrasting descriptive sentence, such as:

Brasilia es una ciudad nueva.   Brasilia is a new city.

The second player, if he has contrasted correctly, then gives another descriptive sentence, for which the first team must supply a contrast, and teams continue alternating in this way. Each team tries to answer as quickly and accurately as possible. If a player's answer is not correct, another member of his own team may try, until a correct sentence has been given. A new sentence may not be introduced except by a player who has responded correctly to the previous sentence. The teacher acts as moderator, deciding whether a player has answered correctly before the game may continue.

ADIVINANZA

Yendo yo para el mercado, me encontré con siete mujeres, cada mujer con siete sacos, en cada saco siete gatos. Entre gatos, sacos y mujeres, ¿cuántos íbamos para el mercado?

(Sólo yo iba al mercado.)

¿CUANDO?

(When?)

Needed: slips of paper and a box or bag.

Write on slips of paper the beginning words of sentences, such as: *hoy, ayer, mañana, el mes que viene, anteayer, la semana pasada, el año pasado,* etc.

Each player in turn takes a slip of paper from the box, reads it and uses the word or words in an oral sentence. Another member of the group may make a list of the completed sentences on the board as they are given.

Player 1:
La semana pasada.

La semana pasada llegó mi amigo de Buenos Aires.	Last week my friend arrived from Buenos Aires.

Player 2:
Mañana.

Mañana quisiera ir a la feria.	Tomorrow I would like to go to the fair.

TRABALENGUAS

El hábil Pablo habló bien en las Baleares, ya que es hablador hábil.	The able Pablo spoke well in the Balearics, since he is an able speaker.

TRABALENGUAS

¿Qué precio tienen estos seis racimos de cerezas? Sesenta y seis pesetas.	How much are these six bunches of cherries? Sixty-six pesetas.

CUENTOS DE NUNCA ACABAR

(Stories that never end)

In Spanish-speaking countries, such *cuentos* are told to young children, in a teasing way. Repeating them helps a student acquire fluency.

Students may write their own *cuentos de nunca acabar* as they learn verb forms. When the *cuento* is letter-perfect, a student may try it out on the class, using a partner if desired.

Player 1:

Salí de Córdoba un día y pasé por Santa Fe, y en el camino encontré un letrero . . .	I left Córdoba one day and passed through Santa Fe, and on the road I found a sign . . .

Player 2:

¿Qué decía el letrero?	What did the sign say?

Player 1:

Decía, "Salí de Córdoba un día . . ."	It said, "I left Córdoba one day . . ."

For more advanced students, a lively and diverting variation might be to have the group participate in the creation of the *cuento*. Each student in turn would add a sentence or two to the story, trying to make it as complicated as possible.

ADIVINANZA

Cien damas en un castillo, todas visten de amarillo.	A hundred ladies in a castle all dressed in yellow.
(La naranja)	(The orange)

ADIVINANZA

Tengo cabeza redonda sin nariz, ojos ni frente, y mi cuerpo se compone tan sólo de blancos dientes.	I have a round head, without nose, eyes, or forehead, and my body is composed of white teeth only.
(La cebolla)	(The onion)

EL ARBOL DE LOS NUMEROS

(The tree of numbers)

An individual or a group may play.

A large tree is drawn on the blackboard. At the end of each branch is a box containing the word for a number, as here:

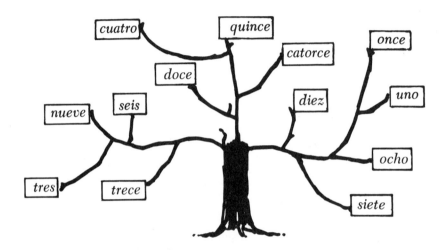

The object of the game is to see who can add the total of the leaves most quickly and accurately. The class may be divided into teams for a contest for the best mathematician in the class. The teacher changes the numbers of the leaves as the game proceeds, to see who can reach the new total first.

Another variation is to have the class find the total of the leaves and then, by erasing the numbers one by one, ascertain the new total.

ADIVINANZA

Tengo calor y frío
y no frío sin calor.
(El sartén)

This a play on words: *frío*
means *cold* or *I fry.*
(The skillet)

QUIERO PRESENTARLES A MI AMIGO . . .

(I want to introduce you to my friend . . .)

Up to 20 may play.

A player goes to the blackboard and says:

Quiero presentarles a mi amigo Paco.

He then writes on the board the letters of the name of his friend, in this manner:

P   A   C   O

In a given time, students must write as many words as they can beginning with each letter of the name, as here:

para	*año*	*coche*	*o*
por	*Ana*	*con*	*ola*
pirámide	*al*	*contar*	*oso*
plátano	*ala*	*correr*	*olé*
	así		

The teacher may set the rules for what kind of words are acceptable, such as only one form of a given verb, no proper names, etc. The player with the longest list of words, after a given time limit, is declared the winner. If there is more time, another introduction and word list may be made in the same way.

ADIVINANZA

Cajita, cajita de buen parecer,	Little box, that looks so nice,
ningún carpintero la ha podido hacer.	No carpenter has been able to make it.
(el huevo)	(The egg)

CATEGORIAS

(Categories)

Any number may play.

Needed: A diagram, on the blackboard, or on mimeographed sheets prepared in advance. A sample diagram may look like this:

	C	L	A	S	E
Nombre de muchacho	Carlos	Luis	Arturo	Santiago	Esteban
Nombre de muchacha	Concha	Lola Luisa Laura	Ana Angela	Sara Sol	Elena
Alimento	carne	leche lechuga	almendra arroz	sopa	ensalada enchilada
La clase	cuaderno	lápiz	aritmética	silla	escritorio
Países	Canadá Costa Rica	Libanesa (República)	Andorra	Suiza Suecia	España Ecuador

The number of vertical columns will depend on the number of letters in the chosen word across the top, but the number of horizontal rows should remain constant, according to the number of categories selected. Many other categories, in addition to those shown on the sample, may be used. Each player must fill in as many words as possible in each space within an allotted time. The one with the most words is the winner.

SE QUITA LA PRIMERA LETRA

(Take away the first letter)

Any number may play.

The purpose of the game is to see how many words each player can write within a given period of time, in this manner:

sola - ola	*creo - reo*
daño - año	*brío - río*

Each player writes a word and forms another word by "decapitating" the first one. The player with the greatest number of correct words is the winner. If he writes a non-existent word, he forfeits two points, and scores one point for each correct word.

Another game is to choose a word or phrase or sentence whose letters may be rearranged in order to form new Spanish words. The player with the longest list of correct words is the winner. Remind students that *ll*, *rr*, and *ch* are all single letters and may not be separated in forming other words.

Example: *sola—sol, ola, la, las, osa,* etc.

Mi coche no funciona.—mi, coche, chico, fecha, etc.

LO QUE VIVE

(The living)

An individual or a group may play.

On the blackboard is printed the word VIDA, in this manner:

V   I   D   A

The object of the game is to see how many living things or persons may be written under each letter of the word. Students may use a dictionary and proper names may be written. The longest list, after a given time, is the winner.

REGALOS PARA MAMA EN EL DIA DE LAS MADRES

(Gifts for Mother on Mother's Day)

Any number may play.

In the same way as above, the word MADRE is printed. Players are to fill the space under each letter with the names of as many gifts as they can find. Each gift must begin with the letter under which it appears, of course. Some unusual gifts may be chosen for humorous effect.

EL PUENTE MAS LARGO

(The longest bridge)

Any number may play.

The Leader writes on the blackboard two letters, such as *e* and *o*. These are the first and last letters of the word that the students are to form. A student may write *extraordinario*, or *escritorio*, or *efectivo*. Each student is trying to make the longest word he can with the two letters. After a given time limit, the Leader writes another pair of letters, and the game continues. The student with the largest number of letters in the final list of words is the winner. All words must be spelled correctly to score.

LAS PALABRAS MAS ALTAS

(The tallest words)

The game is played in the same manner as above, except that first and last letters, and those that will be filled in between, are written in a vertical column. The student with the "tallest" words is the winner.

EL TRIANGULO O PIRAMIDE
(The triangle or pyramid)

Choose a Spanish word that begins with *a*, for example, *alimento*. Draw a triangle with the first letter, *a*, as the apex. Then write the other letters of the word vertically down to the base, in this manner:

As you go down the
triangle, each word,
beginning with the
letter indicated,
should be larger by
one letter than the last one.

$$
\begin{array}{l}
a \\
l\text{-}o \\
i\text{-}r\text{-}a \\
m\text{-}o\text{-}d\text{-}a \\
e\text{-}n\text{-}t\text{-}r\text{-}a \\
n\text{-}e\text{-}v\text{-}a\text{-}d\text{-}a \\
t\text{-}o\text{-}r\text{-}t\text{-}i\text{-}ll\text{-}a \\
o\text{-}p\text{-}r\text{-}i\text{-}m\text{-}i\text{-}d\text{-}o
\end{array}
$$

Try the same thing with another word.

Another version.

Make a triangle of six or seven stages. Now fill it with words, each of which ends in the same letter, such as *a*, and each of which grows larger by one letter as you go down to the base.

$$
\begin{array}{c}
a \\
l\,a \\
s\,e\,a \\
n\,a\,d\,a \\
h\,a\,b\,l\,a \\
c\,o\,m\,e\,t\,a
\end{array}
$$

TRABALENGUAS

Claudio clavó un clavo,	Claudio nailed a nail,
un clavo clavó Claudio.	a nail Claudio did nail.

¿QUE VA A COMER EL PROFESOR SOLIS?

(What is Professor Solís going to eat?)

Any number may play, to acquire vocabulary practice.

Needed: Copies of the list of foods for each player.

Explain to the players that Professor Solís, a bachelor, is so busy with his classes that sometimes he forgets to eat. He lives in a country where it is the custom to have a light breakfast, dinner at 1 p.m., and a light supper in the evening. Tell the students they are to list the foods correctly under *desayuno* (breakfast), *comida* (dinner), or *cena* (supper). The first one to list all the foods correctly under the meal wins the game.

List of foods:

huevos (eggs)
café (coffee)
té (tea)
pan (bread)
carne asada (roast meat)
rosbif (roast beef)
zanahorias (carrots)
apio (celery)
alcachofas (artichokes)
lentejas (lentils)
fresas (strawberries)
leche (milk)
crema (cream)
torta (cake)
panqueques (pancakes)
tocino (bacon)

jamón (ham)
ensalada de lechuga (lettuce salad)
arroz (rice)
mermelada (marmalade)
helado (ice cream)
pan dulce (sweet rolls)
chocolate (chocolate)
sopa de apio (celery soup)
tortillas (tortillas)
pescado (fish)
camarones (shrimp)
flan (custard)
queso (cheese)
naranjas (oranges)
empanadas (meat pies)
sopa de ajo (garlic soup)

Any other foods desired may also be used.

EL VIENTO SOPLO

(The wind blew)

An individual or a group may play this game. It can serve to check knowledge of vocabulary.

Needed: A copy of the list of misplaced articles for each player.

A strong wind indeed must have blown through the town of San Martín. How else could so much merchandise be found in the wrong shops?

Correo de San Martín	Salón de Modas
sobres	harina
tomates en lata	jabón
guantes	faldas
medias	pan dulce
plátanos	sombreros
cartas	

Panadería	Salón de Música
pan	trompeta
zapatos	vestidos
perfume	arpa
medicina	guitarra
azúcar	sopas en lata

Tienda de Abarrotes	Salón de Belleza
manzanas	galletas
frutas en lata	pasteles
piano	polvo para la cara
violoncello	tortas
pelucas	estampillas
pestañas artificiales	

List the shops on a sheet of paper and put each article in its proper shop. If an article might be found in more than one place, the player must list it in both places.

¿CUANTO SABE USTED?

(How much do you know?)

Below are three words in Spanish, all using the same letters of the alphabet. Can you fill in the spaces correctly?

1. __T__ _____ _____ _____

_____ __T__ _____ _____

_____ _____ __T__ _____

2. __A__ _____ _____ _____

_____ __A__ _____ _____

_____ _____ _____ __A__

How many others of the same kind can you make?

Answers: 1. *toro, otro, roto*
2. *acto, taco, toca* or *ando, nado, onda*

TRABALENGUAS

The words do not translate in this one.

Al arzobispo de Constantinopla
  lo quieren desconstantinoplizar.
Al que lo desconstantinople
  se le pagará desconstantinoplizada,
    pues será un buen desconstantinoplizador.

¿CUANTO?

(How much?)

These are some of the kinds of problems found in Spanish arithmetic books. Students may enjoy testing both reading and mathematical skill with them.

1. *Tengo seis manzanas. Le doy dos a Jorge. ¿Cuántas me quedan?*

2. *En una clase con 22 alumnos presentes, hay 4 ausentes. ¿De cuántos alumnos consta la clase entera?*

3. *Si un libro cuesta cinco dólares, ¿cuánto cuesta:*

   1) *la media docena?*
   2) *la docena?*
   3) *el ciento?*

4. *Cuenta de 2 en 2 hasta una docena.*

5. *Cuenta de 2 en 2 hasta veinte.*

6. *45 alumnos y 5 maestros van en excursión al museo. Si cada maestro va acompañado del mismo número de alumnos, ¿cuántos grupos hay y cuántos alumnos hay en cada grupo?*

7. *Mi mamá me envió a la tienda con tres dólares a comprar comestibles. Después de comprar:*

   una docena de huevos @ .67,
   una libra de carne @ .48,
   una libra de queso @ .75, y
   dos libras de frijoles @ .25 la libra,
   ¿cuánto dinero me quedó?

ANSWERS:

¿CUANTO?: 1) 4; 2) 26; 3) 30, 60, 500; 4) 2, 4, 6, 8, 10, 12; 5) 2, 4, 6, 8, 10, 12, 14, 16, 18, 20; 6) *5 grupos de 9 alumnos cada uno;* 7) *60 centavos.*

COMPRA LOCA

(Crazy purchase)

Angelita has to go to market to buy some things. This is her shopping list. She is confused. Can you help her unscramble the words to find out what she is to buy?

rzora   _____

hecel   _____

nairah   _____

voesuh   _____

llavaini   _____

chlocotea   _____

azabalac   _____

allitrtos   _____

aécf   _____

zacúra   _____

Here is a clue. *Todos son comestibles.*

ANSWERS:

arroz, leche, harina, huevos, vainilla, chocolate, calabaza, tortillas, café, azúcar.

EL TESORO DEL PIRATA

(The pirate's treasure)

(Picture of treasure chest opened.)

El pirata dejó un gran tesoro en esta caja. En la caja hay:

1. *un metal de gran valor*
2. *otro metal de gran valor*
3. *joyas verdes*
4. *otras joyas, para la novia*
5. *algo para las orejas*
6. *joyas del mar*
7. *algo para los dedos*
8. *telas finas*

¿Qué cosas serán?

Answers:

1. *oro;* 2. *plata;* 3. *esmeraldas;* 4. *diamantes;*
5. *aretes;* 6. *perlas;* 7. *anillos;* 8. *sedas.*

LOS PARIENTES DE JOSE

(Jose's relatives)

Estos parientes de José acaban de llegar de Asunción para visitarle en la Navidad. (These relatives of Jose have just arrived from Asuncion to visit him at Christmas).

¿Quiénes son?

ita ——————
obeula ——————
baleau ——————
toi ——————
pimra ——————
ormip ——————
ehrmano myaro ——————

Answers:

tía, abuelo, **abuela, tío, prima, primo, hermano mayor.**

EN LA CARRETERA

(On the highway)

Do you know your highway signs? Eight-sided signs always mean stop. Diamond-shaped signs are warnings of a dangerous, or possible dangerous, stretch of road ahead. Crossbucks mark the location of a railroad-highway intersection. Oblong signs give specific rules, speed limits, turning and passing instructions, etc.

Below are some of the words that would be found on road signs in Mexico. Make a quick sketch opposite each word or phrase showing the shape of the sign used for warning or instruction.

Alto　　　　　　　　　　*Adelante*
Camino cerrado　　　　　*Camino sinuoso*
Cuidado con el tren　　　*Velocidad máxima*
Desviación　　　　　　　*Despacio*
Escuela

LA CASA RIDICULA

(The ridiculous house)

A. *La casa está toda*   The house is disorderly.
   desarreglada.

Answer the questions based on the picture:

1. *¿Dónde está el sofá?* _____

2. *¿Dónde está la cama?* _____

3. *¿Dónde están las flores?* _____

4. *¿Quién está a la puerta?* _____

5. *¿Quién está cazando el gato?* _____

B. *Voy a arreglar la casa.*   I'm going to straighten up
                                the house.

Complete the following statements:

1. *Voy a poner el sofá en* _____

2. *Voy a poner la mesa en* _____

3. *Voy a poner las flores en* _____

4. *Voy a poner el tigre en* _____

5. *Voy a poner la cama en* _____

C. *La casa está en orden.*   The house is in order.

Complete the following sentences:

1. *La mesa está en* _____

2. *La cama está en* _____

3. *El elefante se fue a* _____

4. *El gato está* _____

5. *El sofá está en* _____

MIS LLAVES

(My keys)

Needed: Stiff paper or cardboard; a felt pen; a yarn tie or a metal ring; a punch.

Make two sets of keys, one for "good manners" expressions and the other for useful phrases in conversation. With a felt pen, write on each key the expression desired. Punch a hole in each key and put the keys in the appropriate set, held together with a yarn tie or on a metal ring. They make an attractive decoration for classroom or for student's room at home.

Expressions that may be written on the "good manners" keys are:

Gracias.	*Tenga la bondad.*
Por favor.	*Dispénseme.*
Hágame el favor.	*No hay de que.*
¿Me hace usted el favor?	*Perdóneme usted.*
Con permiso.	*De nada.*

and any others desired.

For the other set of keys with phrases used in conversation, the following expressions may be written on keys:

¿De veras?	*¡No me lo digas!*
¡Qué interesante!	*¡Ya lo creo!*
¡Qué lástima!	*¿Usted cree?*

Puede ser.
or any others desired.

VAMOS A HACER UN CUADERNO ESPECIAL

(Let's make a special notebook.)

Students may enjoy combining a special interest and their study of Spanish vocabulary. Notebooks and scrapbooks might be made, with pictures labeled in Spanish. Some subjects might be:

1. *Los deportes* (Sports)

2. *Mis amigos* (My friends). Snapshots of friends will have appropiate descriptive comments.

3. *Mi hogar* (My home). Draw pictures or use photographs to describe it inside and out.

4. *Mi pueblo* (My town). Draw pictures or maps of places of interest in town.

5. *Las modas* (Fashions). Girls will enjoy making a notebook of fashions at the same time that they learn valuable vocabulary.

EL CALENDARIO

(The calendar)

Students might like to make a large calendar for the wall, marked with the Spanish name for the month at the top and with the days of the week printed in Spanish above the numbers. Make the number spaces large enough so that the weather conditions can be written under each day. Important dates for the class may also be indicated in Spanish on the calendar. Different students may undertake to make the calendar for each month of the school year. The calendar for December might be modeled on this one:

Diciembre						
Domingo	Lunes	Martes	Miércoles	Jueves	Viernes	Sábado
1	2	3	4	5	6	7
8	9	10	11	12	13	14
15	16	17	18	19	20	21
22	23	24	25	26	27	28
29	30	31				

NOTICIAS DEL DIA

(News of the day)

Needed: Newspaper sheet paper; easel or prop on which to hold it; felt pen.

In front of the classroom is placed an easel or poster board holding a large sheet of newsprint paper. At the top of the sheet each day are written the date, a one-line weather report, and news items or announcements of interest to the Spanish class. Each week, the students of a particular row in the classroom take a turn working together and presenting, briefly at the beginning of class, these news items. They will have printed or written the news items on the "newspaper" before the class begins. Each student in the particular row takes a turn reading the news items to the rest of the class.

Here are a few sample news reports and announcements:

Anoche vencimos los Osos 18-14. Los jugadores nuestros son formidables, ¿verdad?

Last night we defeated the Bears, 18-14. Our players are great, aren't they?

Luisa Maldonado se va a Nueva York el 21 de febrero. Adiós, Luisa, y buena suerte.

Luisa Maldonado is going to New York on February 21. Goodbye, Luisa, and good luck.

No se olviden del gran baile el sábado que viene a las nueve.

Don't forget the big dance this coming Saturday at nine.

ADIVINANZA

Una señorita, después de bailar en un salón, va a sentarse en un rincón.

A young lady, after dancing in a room, goes to sit in a corner.

(La escoba)

(The broom)

LOS DIALOGOS
(Dialogues)

A series of dialogues may be carried out. One, called *Los anuncios*, might be done in this manner. An advertising sheet from a newspaper in Spanish is displayed before the group. The players form pairs and each pair selects an ad, one pretending to be the person who placed the ad, and the other player, the one answering it. Each pair works out a dialogue and, when ready, presents it to the group. The ad may be from the classified page, offering various articles for sale, a room or an apartment for rent, or indicating an article lost or found.

DE MEMORIA

(From memory)

Many persons have found that one of the best ways to acquire fluency in a language is to learn by heart some lines of poetry. Great beauty, as well as simplicity, is found in the Spanish poetry of such writers as Juan Ramón Jiménez, Bécquer, Gabriela Mistral, and García Lorca, to name but a few. The recitation is never given until the student feels he is letter-perfect. Students may wish to take turns reciting a brief poem before a group. Then a vote may be taken by the audience for the most pleasing performance.

CONTANDO DE MEMORIA
(Counting from memory)

Learning the poem helps to learn numbers and to acquire fluency.

A student tries to recite the poem from memory and goes as far as he can. If he misses or mispronounces a word, someone else takes his place and continues:

Yo soy el farolero	I am the lamplighter
de la Puerta del Sol;	of the Gate of the Sun;
subo la escalera	I climb the ladder
y enciendo el farol;	and light the lamp;

luego que lo enciendo,	When I light it,
me pongo a cantar;	I begin to sing;
dos y dos son cuatro,	2 and 2 are 4,
cuatro y dos son seis,	4 and 2 are 6,
seis y dos son ocho,	6 and 2 are 8,
ocho y ocho, dieciséis,	8 and 8, 16
y ocho, veinticuatro,	and 8, 24,
y ocho, treinta y dos,	and 8, 32,
más diez que añado,	plus 10 that I add,
son cuarenta y dos.	makes 42.

EL ALFABETO

(The alphabet)

Students like to chant these rhymes in chorus, to learn the correct sound of vowels and consonants.

EL PATIO DE MI CASA

El patio de mi casa es	The patio of my house is
muy particular:	very special; when it rains
cuando llueve se moja	it gets wet just like the others.
igual que los demás.	

H - I - J - K - L - Ll - M - A

Que si tú no me quieres,	If you don't like me, some
otro amigo me querrá.	other friend will like me.

H - I - J - K - L - Ll - M - O

Que si tú no me quieres,	If you don't like me, I'll get
otro amigo tendré yo.	another friend.

A - B - C - D

La burra se me fue	The burro ran away from me
por la calle de tía Merced.	down Aunt Merced's street.

a - e - i - o - u

El burro sabe más que tú.	The donkey knows more than you.

A - E - I - O - U

Arbolito del Perú.	Little tree of Peru.
Yo tengo nueve años.	I am nine years old.
¿Cuántos años tienes tú?	How old are you?

A - E - I - O - U

Yo me llamo María.	My name is María.
¿Cómo te llamas tú?	What's your name?

E, E, E, me gusta el café;
E, E, E, me gusta mucho el
* café;*
* yo no sé si tomaré*
* o si lo dejaré. E, E, E.*

EL GOLF

(Golf)

Needed: A Spanish reader of any kind.

Number lines from one to nine on a paper. Open the book to a page selected at random. Copy opposite each number on your paper the first two letters of the first nine lines of the Spanish text. When each of the nine *hoyos* (holes) of the golf course has two letters beside it, you are ready to play the course.

To the two letters for *hoyo* 1 (such as *r* and *o*), add others before, after, or in between to make the shortest word possible. When you have written a word for *hoyo* 1, go on to *hoyo* 2, and so on around the course, trying to complete the nine holes in as few strokes as possible, that is, having as few letters as possible in the words for each hole.

✿ ✿ ✿ ✿ ✿

Try to play an eighteen-hole match, proceeding in the same manner, with the first two letters of the first eighteen lines of the book.

ANAGRAMAS

(Anagrams)

From two to ten persons may play.

Needed: A *Scrabble* set,° to which have been added the additional letters of the Spanish alphabet. On cardboard squares the same size as the other letters, print: ñ (6), *ll* (10), *rr* (10) and *ch* (12). Two or three squares for each letter should be made.

The game may be played according to the rules supplied with the English game, except that all words must be Spanish, and single letters, such as *c* and *h,* may not be combined to form a single Spanish letter. Scoring follows English rules. The teacher or the players may make other rules concerning formation of words, if desired. For example, they may choose to make illegal the forming of new words by adding *n* or *r* or *s* to a third singular verb, as *habla-hablar,* or by making singular nouns or adjectives plural.

❋   ❋   ❋   ❋   ❋

Another way to play.

The squares are placed, face down, in the center of the table. The first player draws four squares and turns them face up in front of him. If he can, he spells a word of at least three letters. He then draws another square. If he can add this letter to his word, he does so, and continues to draw as long as he can form a new word with each letter. When he cannot use the letter he draws, he places it face up in the center of the table. The next player then draws four letters. He is also permitted to pick up the letter that the first player discarded if he can use it to form a word. He, too, draws as long as he can use the letters to form a word. The game continues with each player in turn. Players may use any of the discarded letters in the center in forming their words.

A player is also permitted to "steal" a word from another player by adding one of his own letters to it. It is not permitted to steal a word by making it plural. For example, if a player has the word *ola*, no one may steal it by making it into *olas*, but it can be stolen by making it *sola*.

A player is permitted to change or lengthen any of his own words by adding *s* or any other letter or letters from the center or the discard pile. For example: *brazo—brazos* or *abrazo, toro—toreo* or *torno* or *trono*. But he can steal a word only with a turned-down letter that he has drawn, not with one from the discard pile.

A time limit can be set for making a word, usually about a minute, or less, if desired.

The winner is the player who makes and keeps ten words first.

*Spanish edition of *Scrabble* is now available in this country.

LA LOTERIA
(Lottery)

Lottery, or Bingo or Lotto as it is called in the United States is very popular in the small towns of Mexico. No special materials are needed to play American-style Bingo in Spanish, but students might enjoy making *Lotería* cards such as are used in the villages south of the border. The cards have pictures of animals, flowers, musical instruments, or even Death and the Devil. Players cover the pictures that are called with *frijoles* (beans) and call out "*Lotería, ¡lo tengo!*" when they have filled the appropriate number of spaces.

Students can make their own *Lotería* cards of stiff cardboard, putting numbers on one side if they wish (for Bingo), and filling the squares on the reverse side with pictures cut from magazines or newspapers. The Leader's card should, of course, be large enough to have spaces for all the numbers in sequence on one side, and all the pictures on the other. Players' cards will have only part of the numbers and pictures and no two cards should be exactly the same. Small pieces of cardboard should be made for all the numbers and all the pictures. Buttons, bottle caps, or circles or squares of cardboard may be used for marking the players' cards.

TRABALENGUAS

The following must be spoken as quickly as possible in only one breath. The person who can reach the highest number of eggs before he runs out of breath is the winner.

La gallina Nicaragua puso un huevo en el altar. Puso uno, puso dos, puso tres, puso cuatro, etc.	The hen Nicaragua laid an egg on the altar. She laid one, she laid two, she laid three, etc.

II Games and activities for the Spanish club

TOCO

(I touch)

Two teams of players may play.

Players from each side take turns naming correctly as many objects as possible in the room. The first player on the team of *Los Gavilanes* picks up a pencil for example, and says:

Toco el lápiz.   I touch the pencil.

He turns to the first player on the other team, *Las Aguilas*, and asks:

¿Qué tocas tú?   What do you touch?

The first player on the other team picks up another object and says:

Toco el libro verde.   I touch the green book.

Turning to the second player on *Los Gavilanes*, he asks:

¿Qué tocas tú?

And the game continues. The team with the largest number of objects correctly named is the winner. If a player mispronounces a word, or fails to name an object within an allotted time, or names an object which has already been touched, a point is given to the opposing team. A referee keeps score for the teams.

Another way to play the game.

In order to show that *toco* also means *I play* (a musical instrument), players may pretend that they are playing musical instruments, and go through the motions, using the same pattern of dialogue:

Player 1:
  Toco el violín.   I play the violin.
  ¿Qué tocas tú?   What do you play?

Player on opposite team:
  Toco la guitarra.   *¿Qué tocas tú?*

¡ARRIBA EL PESO!

(Lift up the peso.)

Two teams of players.

Needed: A long bare table and a Mexican *peso* or a quarter.

Players are divided equally on two sides of the table. One side takes the coin and passes it from one hand to another beneath the table, as the leader of the other team counts:

Uno, dos, tres, cuatro,
cinco, seis, siete, ocho,
nueve, diez. ¡Arriba!   . . . Up!

At the last word, each player on the other side raises his hands above the table, with fists clenched. The leader then calls:

¡Abajo!   ¡Down!

Players slap hands down against the table, open, so that the coin is heard as it strikes the table. The leader of the other team asks his men:

¿Quién tiene el peso   Who has the coin?
(la moneda)?

They indicate the one they suspect of having the coin and their leader orders him:

Levántese las manos.   Raise your hands.

If he does not have the coin, another suspect is indicated and the order is repeated until the coin is revealed. If the coin appears before all the players on the side have been ordered to raise their hands, the coin goes over to the other side to hide and the game continues in the same way.

If the piece of money is not discovered until the last hand has been raised, the first team has the privilege of hiding it again.

TRABALENGUAS

En un plato tres tristes   In a plate three sad tigers
tigres toman té y trigo.   take tea and wheat.

BOLICHES

(Bowling)

Up to 40 may play.

Needed: Small bowling pins, with numbers up to 10 marked on them with a felt pen. A ball.

The pins are set at a distance agreed upon. Players take turns sending the ball toward the pins. The player's score is registered by adding the numbers on the pins he knocks down. The group adds each player's score aloud, in this manner:

Jorge—cinco y siete son doce.   George, 5 and 7 are 12.

Manuel—nueve, dos y tres son catorce.   Manuel, 9, 2, and 3 are 14.

Ana—un estrike—cincuenta y cinco.   Ana, strike, 55.

The game continues in this way for each player in turn.

JUEGO DE PRENDAS

(Forfeits game)

Any number may play.

Needed: Several small articles for each player such as a coin, a hairbow, an old key, a pencil—any trifle that a player is willing to give up and that might not be returned to him. A record player and a few recordings of Spanish songs. A plastic bowl.

The Leader explains that a circle will be formed. A Spanish song familiar to the group will be played while an empty plastic bowl is passed around by the players in the circle. When the music stops, the person who holds the bowl must show the others what his forfeit is and name it in Spanish. The music is resumed and the bowl again passed around the circle. When the music stops the player holding the bowl must likewise pay a forfeit. This is repeated a few times. At the end of the song, the player with the bowl holds up the forfeits for the group to see. He keeps as many as he can correctly name in Spanish. The group corrects him in chorus and the unnamed forfeits remain in the bowl to be passed around the circle as before.

Another song is played and the bowl goes around a few more times, with more interruptions. The final player is permitted to keep the forfeits if he names them correctly.

In some versions, a player who has already forfeited something is allowed to name one of the objects in the bowl on his second turn and, if the name is correct, he may take the object out.

MI SECRETO

(My Secret)

Up to 30 may play this guessing game.

Needed: An 8x10 piece of cardboard or stiff paper for each player.

Each player writes on his cardboard the title, *Mi secreto*, and lists below the title about five or six clues. On the back of the cardboard, he writes his secret.

In turn, each player shows his card to the other players and reads aloud the clues, taking care not to show them what is written on the back. For example:

> *Mi secreto*
> *No es muy grande ni muy chico.*
> *La vi en un almacén en el centro.*
> *Me gusta mucho.*
> *Mis padres me la van a regalar.*
> *Tiene cuerdas.*

Those in the group take turns guessing what it is. The one who guesses then takes his card with its secret and shows it to the group. If no one guesses the secret of the first player, he turns the card over and reveals the secret, for example, *una guitarra*.

LA ESCOBA

(The broom)

Any uneven number may play this game from El Salvador.

Needed: A broom. Marching music.

The game begins as the Leader hands the broom to a player. Indicating the broom, the player says:

Tengo la escoba.   I have the broom.

The other players take partners and march around as the music plays. The one with the broom brings up the rear. As they march the Leader gives the players various commands which they obey, such as:

¡Adelante!	Forward!
¡A la derecha!	To the right!
¡A la izquierda!	To the left!
¡Alto!	Halt!

When they have stopped, the Leader gives the command:

¡Escojan otras parejas!   Choose other partners.

The players choose new partners and the one left without a partner takes the broom. The game cannot continue until the player left with the broom says:

Tengo la escoba.   I have the broom.

Once more the players march around to the music until the Leader gives the command to stop. This may also be played as a dancing game. The odd partner has the broom as a partner in a dance.

ADIVINANZA

¿Qué tiene ojo y no ve?   What has an eye and can't see?
(La aguja)   (The needle)

EL CUMPLEAÑOS

(The birthday)

About ten may play.

Needed: Pictures of various gifts with the Spanish name under each picture, if desired.

The players form a circle and sing to the tune of "Happy Birthday to You":

Felicidades a ti,		*Cumpleaños feliz,*
felicidades a ti,	or	*cumpleaños feliz,*
felicidades a ti,		*cumpleaños feliz,*
felicidades a ti.		*cumpleaños feliz.*

The first player says:

El día de mi cumpleaños, recibí unos dulces.

On my birthday I received some candy.

Player 2:

El día de mi cumpleaños, recibí unos dulces y un disco.

. . . I received some candy and a record.

Player 3:

El día de mi cumpleaños, recibí unos dulces, un disco y un libro.

. . . I received some candy, a record, and a book.

The game continues around the circle. Each player must add one more item to the gift list, repeating all those previously named if he can. Each gift that the player lists counts a point for him and the winner is the one with the most points when the game ends.

¿HAN VISTO A MI AMIGO?

(Have you seen my friend?)

This traditional game of Chile is suitable for 15 or 20 players.

Players form a line, one behind the other. The first in line, the Leader, is blindfolded. The Leader asks:

¿Han visto a mi amigo?

Others:
No, señor.	No, sir.

Leader:
¿Saben dónde está mi amigo?	Do you know where my friend is?

Others:
Sí, señor.

The Leader goes forward, taking eight slow steps. While he is doing this, the others quickly change their places, moving forward or backward, as they wish. One of the players takes his place as second in line, in back of the Leader, who keeps his back turned. The other players ask the Leader:

¿Quién es?	Who is it?

The Leader tries to guess who is standing directly in back of him. He is permitted three questions before he is obliged to name someone, for example:

¿Es chico o chica?	Is it a boy or girl?

Others:
Es chica.

Leader:
¿Es alta?	Is she tall?

Others:
No, es baja.	No, she is short.

Leader:

   ¿Es morena con ojos negros?   Is she a dark-eyed brunette?

Others:

   No, es rubia con ojos azules.   No, she's a blue-eyed blonde.

Leader:

   ¿Es Margarita?

If the Leader's guess is correct, he is given another turn. If his guess is incorrect, another player takes his place.

SIGA AL LIDER
(Follow the leader.)

   Any number may play.

   The group follows the Leader, in a line, chanting:

Siga al líder,	Follow the leader,
sígale bien.	follow him well.
Lo que hace él,	What he does,
haremos también.	we too will do.

   The Leader may have the players follow his motions; he may have a "Conga" line; or he may have players pause in their singing of the verse to count with him in Spanish or to repeat the lines of a rhyme or verse of a Spanish song.

¡ADELANTE!
(Go forward!)

   Any number may play. One player is "It."

   One person stands in the middle of the room, facing the group. He wants to get to the other side of the room. The group asks him questions, in turn, but only questions which can be answered by "*sí*" or "*no.*" When the player can answer "*sí*" to the question, he may take one step forward. When he must answer "*no,*" he must take one step backward. The number and variety of questions asked depend on the players' Spanish vocabulary. A few sample questions might be:

¿Vive usted en California?	Do you live in California?
¿Va usted a casa?	Are you going home?
¿Le gusta el beisbol?	Do you like baseball?

¿QUE COSA SE CAYO?
(What fell?)

About 35 may play.

Needed: About 10 objects that can be dropped without breaking, a carton for them. Suggested objects: *un cuchillo* (knife), *dos tenedores* (two forks), *tres cucharas* (three spoons), *un zapato* (shoe), etc.

The players turn their backs and listen as the Leader takes each article from the carton and drops it to the floor. To introduce the players to the game, the Leader may drop a knife, and say:

El número uno.	Number one.
¿Se cayó . . . un tenedor?	Did a fork, spoon, or knife fall?
una cuchara? un cuchillo?	

The players list opposite 1 on their papers the name of the object they believe was dropped. The Leader proceeds with another object, each time naming several choices for what was dropped. At the end of the game, the players turn around and face the Leader with their lists. Quickly the Leader repeats the dropping of the articles, now seen, naming aloud each object so that players may check their lists. The one with the most correct answers wins. The game may also be played with oral answers instead of written ones.

¡SALVESE QUIEN PUEDA!

(Save yourself, whoever can!)

20 to 30 players.

The players form a line about 30 steps from a wall or something that will serve as "base." They turn their backs to the base and face the Leader who stands a little distance from them. The Leader tells any story (about a shipwreck, a storm, a disaster, etc.), but it must end with the words "¡Sálvese quien pueda!". When the players hear the word *pueda*, they must turn and run to touch base. Whoever reaches base last, or fails to get there, takes the place of the Leader and the game continues.

Permission to reprint given by *Asociación Cristiana Femenina*, México, D.F., México.

UN PASEO AGRADABLE

(A pleasant stroll)

Any number may play.

One player is chosen to be "It" *(El)* and the others, taking hands, form a circle about him and say or sing:

Has tenido un lindo paseo,	You've had a pretty stroll,
con muchas cosas gozaste.	you enjoyed many things.
Cumpliremos con tu deseo	We'll comply with your wish
de adivinar lo que miraste.	to guess what you saw.

The one in the circle pantomimes what he has seen on his way, such as a man fishing in a boat, a woman walking her dog, a boy playing ball, etc. The other players try to guess what it is, each one taking a turn.

Adapted from *Libro de Juegos*, page 19. Permission to reprint granted by World Bureau Office of the World Association of Girl Guides and Girl Scouts, New York City.

¿QUE TRAJISTE PARA EL DIA DE CAMPO?

(What did you bring for the picnic?)

Any number may play.

Needed: A large box or bag.

Each player takes a turn bringing forth from the box a make-believe object for the picnic, and pantomiming what it is. The others in the group try to guess from the player's motions what the article is.

All (to Player 1):
   ¿Qué trajiste?   What did you bring?

Player 1:
   Traje . . .   I brought . . .

He goes through the motions of taking out, for example, a ball.

All:
   ¿Qué será? No sé. Yo no   What can it be? I don't know.
   sé. ¿Qué será? . . .   . . .

One Player:
   ¿Es una pelota?   Is it a ball?

Player 1:
   Sí, es pelota.

The player who guessed now becomes the new pantomimer, and the game continues in the same manner.

ADIVINANZA

Platillo, platillo,   Little plate, little plate
platillo de avellanas,   little plate of hazelnuts,
por el día se recogen,   they are gathered by day
por la noche se derraman. and scattered by night.

(Las estrellas)   (The stars)

LOS REGALOS INVISIBLES

(Invisible gifts)

20 to 30 may play this game.

Needed: Slips of paper on which are written the names of some unlikely gifts, at least as many as there are players. They might include such things as:

una bicicleta para dos personas	a bicycle for two
un jardín zoológico	a zoo
un tren	a train
un camello	a camel
una corona de oro	a gold crown
un circo	a circus

or others, the more fantastic the better.

Without showing the slips, the Leader puts them in a box or hat. The players take turns taking slips of paper from the box and then, in turn, pantomime to the others their unlikely gift. As each player pantomimes, the others try to guess.

ENFRENTE DE MI CASA . . .

(In front of my house . . .)

Any number may play.

A group of players form a large circle around one who is "It" *(El)*. He begins the game by saying:

Enfrente de mi casa . . .

Others:

¿Qué viste?	What did you see?

El then acts out what he saw happen in front of his house. The players in the circle take turns trying to guess:

¿Dos niñas jugando?	Two little girls playing?

El (repeats guess and demonstrates again):
  ¿Dos niñas jugando? No.

Another player:
  ¿Dos muchachos peleando?   Two boys fighting?

El:
  ¿Dos muchachos peleando? No.

The game continues until the players in the circle either guess the action or give up, saying:

Nos damos por vencidos.	We give up.

El:

Un niño perdido llorando,	A lost child crying and a
y un joven que le dijo:	young man who said to him:
"No llores. Yo te ayudo."	"Don't cry. I'll help you."

Whenever a person in the circle guesses the action or they give up, a new *El* is chosen and the game continues.

HACEMOS UNA LOCURA

(We are doing something crazy.)

Any number may play, divided into several small groups.

One group secretly decides on an action which they will pantomime in a comical manner. Then they say to the rest of the group:

Estamos listos.	We are ready.

Others:

¿Qué hacen ustedes?	What are you doing?

Group 1:
  Hacemos una locura.

Others:
A ver.   Let's see.

The small group may pantomime that they are: en route to Mars, scientists in the Antarctic, football players, employees held up by a bank robber, etc. The more ridiculous the pantomime, the more fun the game is. The others try to guess. If their guesses are partially right, the group encourages them with:

¿Qué más?   What else?

One player:
Son empleados en un
    banco . . .   You are bank employees . . .

Group:
¿Qué más?

Another player:
. . . entra un ladrón . . .   A robber enters . . .

Group:
¿Qué más?

Another player:
. . . y todos corren
    asustados.   . . . And all run scared.

Group:
Sí, eso es.   Yes, that's it.

Or, after a suitable effort, the other players may say:

Nos damos por vencidos.   We give up.

Then the group explains what they are doing and another group takes a turn.

TRABALENGUAS

Yo solo sé una cosa,   I know only one thing,
solo sé que no sé nada.   only that I know nothing.

ACTORES MUDOS

(Silent actors)

Any number may play.

Needed: A list of proverbs, familiar phrases, quotations, prepared on individual slips of paper.

One person is chosen to be the first silent actor. He selects a slip of paper, and then tells the group to which category it belongs, for example:

Es un proverbio.   It is a proverb.

He then goes through the motions of enacting the words on his slip of paper and the others take turns guessing what it is he is portraying. The actor shakes his head at incorrect guesses and nods at correct or partially correct ones. When someone has guessed correctly, he changes places with the actor and the game continues.

Adapted from *Juegos Scouts en el Local,* no. 113. Permission granted by Consejo Interamericano de Escultismo, México, D.F., México.

¿QUE DICEN?

(What do they say?)

Two or more groups of players.

Needed: A number of pictures, cut from magazines or newspapers, each showing two or more people in conversation.

Each group is given a picture and told that, within a given time limit, the whole group is to compose a conversation that the persons in the picture might be having. The game may be played by students at various levels of proficiency, with conversations more complex as students gain greater skill. The Leader may also wish to establish a minimum or maximum number of sentences for the conversations. When the time is up, conversations are read to the whole group while each picture is displayed. If there is time, more than one conversation might be attempted.

¿QUE OFICIO TIENE SU PADRE?

(What is your father's occupation?)

20 to 40 may play this game, divided into two equal teams.

The first player on the first team faces the other team and some-one asks him:

¿Qué oficio tiene su padre?

The player must pantomime his father's occupation and his op-ponents have two minutes to try to find out what occupation he is pantomiming. If they are able to guess correctly, the team receives a point; there is no score if they have not guessed cor-rectly within the time limit. The game may proceed with all the players on the first team doing their pantomimes in turn while members of the other team try to guess. Or, if preferred, teams may alternate in pantomiming and guessing. The team with the most points when all players on both sides have performed their pantomimes is the winner.

¿DE DONDE VIENEN?

(Where are you from?)

Up to 40 may play, in two teams.

The two teams face each other, about twenty feet apart. Team A approaches the other group, Team B, saying:

Ya llegamos.   Here we are.

Team B:
¿De dónde vienen?   From where do you come?

Team A:
De Madrid. (or the name of any other city)

Team B:
¿Qué oficio tienen?   What's your job?

Team A pantomimes its occupation, without making it too easy for the other side to guess. They may be balloon salesmen, astronauts, farmers, etc. When the other side has correctly guessed the occupation, the members of Team A run to a marker, pursued by Team B. All those captured must join the other team. The pantomime is then repeated by the other team in the same manner, with a different occupation. Teams may alternate in "doing their act" for as many rounds as desired. When the game ends, the team with the most players is the winner.

CHARADAS
(Team Charades)

Two teams, with 10 or more persons on each team.

Needed: A prepared list of famous people, song titles, book titles, names of movies, etc., arranged by categories, and each single title or name on a slip of paper. A stop watch or watch with a second hand.

Each team member must act out a charade before the rest of his own team, who must try to guess what he is portraying before three minutes have elapsed. The Leader sits in a central place, holding a box containing the slips of paper and a stop watch. The first player on the first team comes up and draws a slip from the box. He must then announce what category he is performing, for example:

El título de un libro.   The title of a book.

The Leader begins timing, and the players on the first team try to guess what he is doing. If they fail to guess within three minutes, he must reveal the name to them, and they get no score. If they succeed, the Leader notes the time elapsed. Then the first player on the second team takes a turn, and teams continue to alternate in this manner until all players have acted out a charade. The team with the shorter total time and the fewer misses is the winner.

EL CUERPO

(The body)

An even number may play, in two teams.

One line of players faces the other, and a player from one team says:

Este es mi dedo—uno, dos, tres, cuatro (up to ten).	This is my finger—one, two, three, four, etc.

Before he reaches ten, a player on the opposite side must point to another part of the body, such as his ear, and say:

Esta es mi oreja—uno, dos, tres, cuatro . . .	This is my ear—one, two, three, four . . .

Another player on the first team must be ready to speak before the second player counts to ten, and the game continues in this manner through both teams. A player who fails to answer in time must drop out and the winning team is the one with more players remaining at the end of the game.

LAS ESTATUAS

(The statues)

As many as 40 may play.

Needed: A variety of objects familiar to the group.

The players line up in two teams, perhaps a boys' and a girls' team, and each one holds some object in his hand. Each team chooses one of its members to be the *estatua* (statue), to stand a short distance from the teams. At a signal from the Leader, the first player on one team runs to the *estatua*, places her in the position desired (a scout gazing into the distance, a dancer in a pose, or anything the team wishes). The first player holds up the object in her hand, gives the Spanish word for it, and places it somewhere about the *estatua,* in her hand, on her head, on the ground, etc.

Then a player from the other team takes a turn and does likewise with his team's *estatua.* He may put a hat on the *estatua's* head, a bunch of flowers in his hand, in an effort to make the *estatua* look funny. He must also name the object in Spanish.

If a player forgets or mispronounces the name of the article, one point is charged against his team. The next player on the other team makes the correction, with help from his team if necessary. The game continues with players taking turns. The Leader keeps score and announces the winning team. The game can be hilarious.

LOS ARTISTAS

(The artists)

15 or 20 may play.

Needed: A picture cut from a magazine or newspaper, a piece of paper, and a pencil for each player. If desired, all the pictures may be of one kind, such as babies, animals, current news photos, cartoons, etc.

Each person is given a picture and pencil and paper. Within a given time limit, he is to write a long descriptive or narrative title for his picture, in Spanish. Students should try to be as imaginative and humorous as possible, and, at the same time, write the most accurate Spanish. When the time is up, students display their pictures and read their captions. If desired, the group may vote on what they consider the best captions.

*   *   *   *   *

In a variation, several student volunteers may prepare pictures for the group. The pictures are displayed in front of the group and each one is told to write a caption for each picture. The group, or judges chosen from within it, can select the best caption for each picture from the various entries.

TIRO AL BLANCO

(Target practice)

The entire class may play the game, as individuals or as teams.

Needed: A heavy piece of corrugated cardboard cut in a circle, and marked out like this:

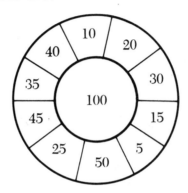

The target is placed on the floor about ten feet away from the players. Players take turns tossing a checker, bottle top, or similar object at the target. Each player must call out in Spanish the number he has scored. If he forgets it or mispronounces it, he gets no score. Any player who scores a bull's eye is given another turn. One player acts as scorekeeper. Teams might like to have names, such as *Los Zorros* (Foxes) and *Los Lobos* (Wolves). At the end of play, the scorekeeper may announce:

¡Los Zorros ganaron!   The Foxes won!

TRABALENGUAS

Si seiscientas sierras asierran   If 600 saws saw 600 series
seiscientas series de cigarros,   of cigars, 606 saws saw
seiscientas seis sierras   606 series of
   asierran   cigars.
seiscientas seis series de
cigarros.

PERSONAJES ILUSTRES

(Famous persons)

Any number of players, divided into two teams.

Needed: Prepare several biographical sketches of well-known personalities, living or dead. Each sketch should consist of a number of fairly short sentences or clues, arranged so that the identity of the personality becomes more obvious with each succeeding statement. Each sentence in the sketch should be numbered and the total written at the top of the page.

The object of the game is for teams to take turns guessing the identity of the famous personality, as each statement about him is read aloud by the Leader. If a member of either team guesses correctly after the first statement is read, his team receives as many points as there are statements in the sketch. As each succeeding statement is read, members of the two teams alternate in guessing, if they can. A point is subtracted from the total score for the sketch as each additional clue is given. For example, if the sketch contains nine clues in all, and a player guesses the personality correctly after the fourth clue is read, his team receives six points. No penalty is attached to a wrong guess; the reading is merely continued until someone guesses correctly.

¿DESEA USTED SER TRADUCTOR?

(Do you want to be a translator?)

Any number of players, divided into two teams.

Needed: 3 x 5 cards on which are written the titles of Spanish-language songs.

Players form two lines. The first player in one line is handed a card with a song title on it. He must pronounce the title and then give a correct English translation of it. If his answer is correct—allowing for a fairly free translation—he scores one point for his team. He then goes to the back of his line, and the first player in the other line is given a card and repeats the procedure. The game continues until all the players have had one turn or until all the cards are used. Below are some song titles that may be used. Of course, others may be added.

Amé y perdí	*Carta perdida*
Ayer salí de la cárcel	*Cuatro cartas*
Al baile me fui	*Corrido de Kennedy*
Ay cariño	*Doctora Corazón*
Adiós a Pedro Armendáriz	*Dios me señaló*
América de luto	*De puro ardor*
Allá	*Desolación*
Al fin mujer	*De dónde vienes paloma*
Amor sin medida	*Estoy en tu boda*
Aunque tengas razón	*Esta tristeza mía*
Ando como bala	*El pecador*
Amores por correo	*En tu día*
Aquella herida	*El precio de tu cariño*
Bésame y olvídame	*Esclavo y amo*
Besos de papel	*El patas blancas*
Cartero amigo	*El huérfano*
Canción de un preso	*El burro norteño*
Cuando despierto	*El día de tu boda*
Cuando dos almas	*Gaviota traidora*
Chiquita pero picosa	*Has de pagar*
Copa vaciá	*La tumba abandonada*
Cuando te miro	*La mal agradecida*

TRABALENGUAS

Pedro Pablo Pérez Peña,
    pobre pintor portugués,
    pinta paisajes por poco precio,
    para poder pasar pronto para París.

Pedro Pablo Pérez Peña,
    poor Portuguese painter,
    paints landscapes for little cost,
    in order to travel soon to Paris.

RIMAS

(Rhymes)

Any number may play.

Needed: A number of cards or slips of paper, on each of which is a pair of rhyming Spanish words.

Each student is given a pair of rhyming words which he is to use in a two-line poem. Allow players a short time limit in which to compose their poems. Then each one, as he is called on, recites his poem for the group.

Some rhyming pairs that might be used are:

fresas - mesas	*canto - santo*
llores - flores	*cadena - morena*
una - luna	*esfera - espera*
luna - laguna	*miel - clavel*
cosa - rosa	*mango - tango*
corazón - razón	*ojo - rojo*
condición - visión	*niña - piña*

❖ ❖ ❖ ❖ ❖

Students also might enjoy making their own rhyming pairs and challenging each other to make couplets of them.

TRABALENGUAS

Erre con erre cigarro,	R with R cigar,
erre con erre barril,	R with R barrel,
rápidos ruedan los carros	rapidly roll the cars
cargados de azúcar del	loaded with sugar from
ferrocarril.	the railroad.

III Let's plan a party

These two simple games would be suitable for initiation stunts for new club members.

FALTA EL SUJETO

(The subject is missing.)

Any number may play.

Needed: A number of cards or slips of paper, on each of which is written only the predicate of a sentence. One slip for each player.

The slips of paper are placed in a container. Players may sit in a circle around the container. Each player, in turn, must go to the container and draw a slip, read the half-sentence that is written on it and, adding a subject, repeat the sentence correctly. For example:

. . . *son hermanos.*
Pepe y Juan son hermanos.

The game continues until each player has drawn a slip and completed a sentence.

LAS FRASES INCOMPLETAS

(Incomplete sentences)

Needed: Slips of paper or cards on which are written only subjects of sentences. One for each player.

The procedure is exactly the same as for the previous game. In this case the player reads aloud the subject and supplies a predicate for it.

TRABALENGUAS

These make amusing stunts for a party or initiation. The following one is a tonguet twister to end all tongue twisters.

En la ciudad de Pamplona
* hay una plaza,*   In Pamplona is a plaza,
en la plaza hay una esquina,   in the plaza is a corner,
en la esquina hay una casa,   on the corner is a house,
en la casa hay una sala,   in the house is a room,
en la sala hay una alcoba,   in the room is an alcove,
en la alcoba hay una cama,   in the alcove is a bed,
en la cama hay una mesa,   on the bed is a table,
en la mesa hay una jaula,   on the table is a cage,
en la jaula hay una estaca,   in the cage is a stick,
en la estaca hay una lora,   on the stick is a parrot,
en la lora hay una pulga.   on the parrot is a flea.

Now try backwards:

La pulga en la lora,
la lora en la estaca,
la estaca en la jaula,
la jaula en la mesa,
la mesa en la cama,
la cama en la alcoba,
la alcoba en la sala,
la sala en la casa,
la casa en la esquina,
la esquina en la plaza,
la plaza en la ciudad de Pamplona.

TRABALENGUAS

La bailarina baila como una   The dancer dances like a
* ballena, porque va llena*   whale because she is
* de avellanas.*   full of hazelnuts.

PALABRAS QUE SE HACEN PAREJAS

(Words that make pairs)

Any number may play.

Needed: Pairs of contrasting words, printed on cards, such as: *frío - caliente.* Sort the cards into two piles, A and B, so that for each word in group A there is a contrasting word in group B.

Each player is given one of the cards from group A. When everyone has a card, the Leader begins to read the words on the cards in group B, one by one. When he hears the word that contrasts with the one on his card, a player should call out the word on his card as quickly as he can. The Leader should go very rapidly through the pile of B cards, trying to catch the players unawares, in this manner:

¡Caliente—una vez!	Hot—once,
¡caliente—dos . . .	hot—twice! . .
Player: (holding up his card):	
¡Frío!	Cold!

Leader (puts B card face down in a pile):	
¡Frío—pareja hecha!	Cold—pair complete!
¡Invierno—una vez!	Winter—once,
¡Invierno—dos veces!	Winter—twice!
¡Invierno—no hay!	Winter—not here!

If the player who holds *verano* does not reply before the Leader has said the word on the B card three times—rapidly—the B card is placed face up on another pile. When all the cards in the B group have been read, any player whose contrasting B card is face up must pay a forfeit or perform some stunt as a penalty.

MATA-RILI-RILI-RON

This is one of the most popular of the traditional games in Spanish-speaking countries.

The boys form a line facing the girls. As one group speaks or sings, all take a few steps forward, then backward.

Muchachos:
Muy buen día, su señoría, *Mata-rili-rili-ron.*	A very good day, your Ladyship, . . .

Muchachas:
¿Qué querría su señorío? *Mata-rili-rili-ron.*	What would your Lordship like?

Muchachos:
Yo querría a una de sus hijas. *Mata-rili-rili-ron.*	I would like one of your daughters.

Muchachas:
¿A cuál de ellas usted querría? *Mata-rili-rili-ron.*	Which one would you like?

Muchachos:
Yo querría a Rosita. *Mata-rili-rili-ron.*	I would like Rosita.

Muchachas:
¿En qué oficio la pondremos? *Mata-rili-rili-ron.*	In what job shall we place her?

Muchachos:
La pondremos de planchadora. *Mata-rili-rili-ron.*	We'll put her to work ironing.

Muchachas:
Ese oficio no le agrada. *Mata-rili-rili-ron.*	She doesn't like that job.

Muchachos:
   La pondremos bailarina.   We'll have her be a dancer.
   Mata-rili-rili-ron.

Todos:
   Celebramos la fiesta todos.   We'll all celebrate the fiesta.
   Mata-rili-rili-ron.

LOS PROVERBIOS QUEBRADOS

(Broken proverbs)

Another good mixer for a party.

Needed: On stiff paper write a number of proverbs, one for each piece of paper. Then cut each paper in two so that only half of the proverb is on each piece. There should be about half as many proverbs as there are players.

As each player arrives he is handed one of the halves of a proverb. He must then circulate around until he finds who has the half that completes his proverb. When all players have been given a half-proverb, give them time to circulate, then read—from a list of complete proverbs—the correct matchings, in case there should be confusion as to how they are to be matched. This game provides an interesting way to select partners for a dinner party or later games.

TRABALENGUAS

Me han dicho que has dicho   They said that you said
   un dicho,   a saying,

que han dicho que he dicho   that they said I said,
   yo,

el que lo ha dicho mintió.   the one who said that lied.

EL PERICO

(The parrot)

Characters: Parrot seller, her daughter, *Jóvenes*.

Needed: Several small paper parrots or pictures of parrots. A rose.

Parrot Seller:

Yo vendo mis periquitos,	I sell my parrots, they are fine
son finos y muy bonitos.	and pretty.
Los traigo desde Colima y	I bring them from Colima and
vienen muy bien	they are very well taken
cuidados.	care of.

Jóvenes:

Daca, daca, daca, perico;	Give me . . . little parrot.
daca, daca, daca la pata.	Give me . . . your foot.

Parrot Seller:

¿Quién compra mis	
periquitos?	Who will buy my parrots?
Los vendo muy baratitos;	I sell them very cheap.
sus plumas son relucientes,	Their feathers are shiny.
su pico muy encorvado.	Their beaks very curved.

(Points to parrots' feathers and beaks as she speaks).

Jóvenes:

Pica, pica, pica, perico;	Peck . . . little parrot.
pica, pica, pica la rosa.	Peck . . . the rose.

(One of *Jóvenes* extends a rose toward parrot.)

Parrot Seller:

Son finos mis periquitos;	My parrots are fine;
me quedan ya muy	I have only a few left.
poquitos.	
¡Ay, niña!, llévese el suyo.	Child, take yours.

(Parrot Seller coaxes *Jóvenes*, one by one, to buy a parrot.)

Jóvenes:

> *Daca, daca, daca, perico.*
> *Daca, daca, daca la pata.*

Daughter:

Mamita, suerte tuvimos;	Mama, we were lucky.
ya todo, todo vendimos.	We've sold them all.

Parrot Seller:

No queda ni un periquito,	Not a parrot left,
y mira, cuánto dinero.	and look how much money.

Jóvenes:

> *Pica, pica, pica, perico;*
> *pica, pica, pica la rosa.*

From *El Cancionero de la Escuela y del Hogar,* by Leonardo Lis, Editorial Progreso, Mexico, D.F., Mexico, page 50. Permission to reprint granted by publisher.

EL MUSICO AMBULANTE

(The strolling musician)

Characters: Músico (musician), *Jóvenes.*

Needed: Toy violin, guitar, flute, and drum.

Músico:

Soy músico ambulante, y sé	I am a strolling musician,
cantar también;	and I can sing, too.
si quieren escucharme,	If you want to hear me I'll play
violín les tocaré.	a violin for you.

Jóvenes:

> *Sin e sun, sun, sun.*
>   (Repeat 3 more times.)
>   (*Músico* and *Jóvenes* pretend to play violin.)

Músico and Jóvenes:

Mi pieza ya acabé.	I've finished my piece.

  (All put down violins in pantomime.)

Músico:
> Soy músico ambulante, y sé cantar
> también; si quieren escucharme, guitarra
> tocaré.

> . . .

> I'll play the guitar.

Jóvenes:
> Plin, plun, plin, plin, plin.
> (Repeat 3 more times.)

Músico and Jóvenes:
> Mi pieza ya acabé.

Músico:
> Soy músico ambulante, y sé cantar
> también; si quieren escucharme, mi
> flauta tocaré.   I'll play my flute.

Jóvenes:
> Fi, fu, fi, fi, fi.
> (Repeat 3 more times.)

Músico and Jóvenes:
> Mi pieza ya acabé.

Músico:
> Soy músico ambulante, y sé cantar
> también; si quieren escucharme,
> tambor les tocaré.   I'll play the drum for you.

Jóvenes:
> Ra, ta, plan, plan, plan
> (Repeat 3 more times.)

Músico and Jóvenes:
> Mi pieza ya acabé.

From *El Cancionero de la Escuela y del Hogar*, by Leonardo Lis, Editorial Progreso, Mexico, D.F., Mexico, page 50. Permission to reprint granted by publisher.

EL ARBOL DE LA SUERTE

(The luck tree)

Needed: A small artificial tree, in a pot on a table. Slips of paper hung from the branches with colored string, one for each person present. The papers have fortunes written on them, or proverbs, jokes, tongue twisters, or even incomplete sentences or anagrams, or stunts to perform.

Each player takes one of the slips of paper from the tree and reads it before the group. If the papers contain stunts or other feats that must be performed, the player performs as required. The tree lends itself to a variety of uses, all of which are good party mixers.

If students are seated around several tables, for example, at a dinner party, each table may have a tree. The slips on the tree may contain clues to a treasure hunt, written in Spanish, or they may be made like coupons, entitling the bearer to receive some comical gift or fantastic prize.

¿DESEA USTED SER POLICIA DE TRAFICO?

(Do you want to be a traffic policeman?)

Characters: Agente de policía, automovilista.

Agente:
> *¿Por qué tanta prisa, señor?* Why the rush, sir? I
> *Tengo que multarlo por* have to fine you for
> *exceso de velocidad. ¿Su* speeding. Your name
> *nombre y dirección?* and address?

Automovilista:
> *Mi nombre:*
> *Constantinoplinito* My name is Constantinoplinito

Atzcapotzalco de Arrellano.
La dirección: esquina de
Popocatépetl e
Iztaccíhuatl.

Atzcapotzalco de Arrellano.
My address: the corner of
Popocatépetl and Iztaccíhuatl.

Agente:
   ¿Cómo?

What?

Automovilista:
   Constantinoplinito
     Atzcapotzalco
   de Arrellano, a sus órdenes.
   La dirección: esquina de
   Popocatépetl e Iztaccíhuatl.

. . . at your
service.

Agente:
   Ajem . . . Mire usted, hoy no
     voy a multarlo, que sea la
     última vez, ¿me entiende?
     ¡La última vez!

Ahem . . . Look, I'm not going
to give you a ticket today, but
let this be the last time, do
you understand?
The last time!

¿DESEA USTED SER MESERO?

(Do you want to be a waiter?)

Characters: Mesero, Hombre, Mujer.

Hombre:
   ¿Qué clase de pastel es
     éste—limón o manzana?

What kind of pie is this—
lemon or apple?

Mesero:
   ¿Qué sabor tiene, señor?

What does it taste like, sir?

Hombre:
   Tiene sabor de lodo.

It tastes like mud.

Mesero:
   Pues, entonces, es pastel

de manzana. El pastel de limón tiene sabor de cemento.	Well, then, it's apple pie. The lemon pie tastes like cement.

✿ ✿ ✿ ✿ ✿

Mujer:
    Una taza de café, por favor,   A cup of coffee, please,
      sin crema.   without cream.

Mesero:
    Nos falta la crema, señora.   We are out of cream, madam.
    ¿Le conviene tomarlo sin   Would you mind taking it
      leche?   without milk?

¿DESEA USTED SER PROFESOR DE ESPAÑOL?

(Do you want to be a professor of Spanish?)

Characters: Profesor, dos Alumnos.

Profesor:
  ¿Habla usted español?

Alumno:
  What? What did you say?

Profesor:
  ¿Habla usted español?

Alumno:
  I don't understand.

Profesor:
  I asked, "Do you speak Spanish?"

Alumno:
  Oh, sí. Perfectamente.

Profesor:
>*¿Por qué es tan breve su composición? Todas las otras composiciones son muy largas.*

Why is your composition so short? All the other compositions are very long.

Alumno 2:
>*Pero, profesor, el título de mi composición es La leche condensada.*

But, Professor, the name of my composition is *Condensed Milk.*

From *Voces de las Americas,* Walter Vincent Kaulfers, Book 1, p. 115. Reprinted with permission of publishers, Henry Holt and Company, New York.

* * * * *

Students may enjoy putting on a puppet show in Spanish, using the above skits or any others that they find suitable. Hand puppets are easily obtainable and no special effects or decorations are needed to put on shows using them.

IV Songs

NARANJA DULCE, LIMON PARTIDO

(Sweet Orange, Cut Lemon)

About 30 may play this game, usually played by girls, and said to have originated in Costa Rica.

Players form a circle with one person in the center. As they walk around they sing:

Naranja dulce,	Sweet orange,
limón partido,	cut lemon,
dame un abrazo	give me an embrace,
que yo te pido.	I beg you.
Si fueran falsos	If my vows
mis juramentos,	were untrue,
en otros tiempos	in time
se olvidarán.	they will be forgotten.

The one in the center sings:

Toca la marcha,	Play the march,
mi pecho llora;	my heart is crying;
Adiós, señora,	Goodbye, señora,
yo ya me voy.	I'm going now.

When the singing is ended, the one in the center goes to someone in the circle, gives her an *abrazo* and they exchange places as the game continues.

Naranja dulce, limón partido

Na -ran-ja   dul - ce,   li - món   par -

ti - do, da-meun a - bra - zo que yo te

pi - do. Si fue-ran   fal - sos mis ju - ra -

men - tos, en o - tros   tiem - pos seol-vi - da -

rán.   To - ca la   mar - cha, mi pe -cho

llo - ra; A - diós, se -ño - ra, yo ya me voy.

ARROZ CON LECHE
(Rice With Milk)

In Venezuela this game is often called *"Arroz con coco"* (Rice with coconut). The version below is played by students of Costa Rica.

Students take hands and form a circle. One player stands in the center. As students walk around they sing:

Arroz con leche,	Rice with milk,
me quiero casar	I want to marry
con una viudita	a little widow
de la capital.	from the Capital.
Que sepa coser,	One who can sew,
que sepa bordar,	who can embroider,
que ponga la mesa	who can set the table
en su santo lugar.	in its holy place.

The player in the center now sings:

Yo soy la viudita,	I am the little widow,
la hija del Rey,	daughter of the King,
que quiero casarme	who wants to marry,
y no hallo con quien.	but can't find anyone to marry.

The other players sing:

Pues, cásate, niña,	Well, marry, my girl,
que yo te daré	and I will give you
zapatos y medias	shoes and stockings,
color de café.	brown in color.

The one in the center points to someone in the circle as she sings each of the following lines:

Contigo, sí,	You I will marry,
contigo, no,	you I won't marry,
contigo, mi vida,	you, my darling,
me casaré yo.	I will marry.

When she reaches the last line, the one she points to as she says the word *yo* now becomes the *viudita* in the center as the game continues as before.

Arroz con leche
Rice with Milk

ME REGALARON UN VIOLIN

(They Gave me a Violin)

Para el día de mi santo   For my birthday
me regalaron un violín.   they gave me a violin.
Yi-ri-yin-yin, el violín,
yi-ri-yi-yin, el violín.
Ay, qué dichosa yo me
    quedé;   Oh, how happy it made me.
ay, qué dichosa yo me quedé.

Para el día de mi santo
me regalaron un tambor.   . . . a drum.
Para-pon-pon, el tambor,
Para-pon-pon, el tambor.
Ay, qué contenta yo me quedé;
ay, qué contenta yo me quedé.

From *Saludos Amigos*, Beginner's Spanish, Teacher's Manual, KQED Instructional Television Service, San Francisco, page 23. Permission to reprint granted by Dr. Manuel Guerra.

Me regalaron un violín

Pa-ra el dí - a de mi san - to me re-ga-
Pa-ra el dí - a de mi san - to me re-ga-
For my birthday they gave me

la - ron un vio - lín. Yi-ri-yin - yin, el vio-
la - ron un tam-bor. Pa-ra-pon - pon, el tam-
a vio-lin.(drum)

lín, yi - ri - yi - yin, el vio -
bor, pa - ra - pon - pon, el tam -

lín. Ay, qué di - cho - sa yo me que -
bor. Ay, qué con - ten - ta yo me que -
Oh, how hap - py it made

dé; ay, qué di - cho - sa yo me que - dé.
dé; ay, qué di - cho - sa yo me que - dé.
me; oh, how happy it made me.

VAPORES Y TAMBORES

(Boats and Drums)

Qué bonito que corre el mar   How beautiful is the sea
debajo de los vapores.   beneath the boats.
Sirena, morena,   Oh, my dark mermaid,
repícame los tambores.   beat the drums for me.

Vapores y tambores

From *Folk Songs and Stories of the Americas*, Pan American Union, Washington, D. C. Permission to reprint granted by the Music Division, Pan American Union.

YO ME VOY

(I am leaving)

Yo me voy, yo me voy	I am leaving, I am leaving,
cuando a mí me dé la gana.	whenever I please.
Yo me vine por un día	I came for a day
y me estuve una semana.	and I have been here a week.

Yo me voy

Yo   me   voy,   yo   me   voy   cuan-do a

mí   me dé   la   ga-na.   Yo me   vi-ne por un

dí - a y me es - tuve u - na se - ma-na.

From *Folk Songs and Stories of the Americas,* Pan American Union, Washington, D. C. Permission to reprint granted by the Music Division, Pan American Union.

PERICA
(Parrot)

Cuando la perica quiere	When Perica wishes
que el perico vaya a misa,	her husband to go to mass,
se levanta bien temprano	she rises very early
y le plancha la camisa.	and irons his shirt.

Refrain:

Ay, mi perica, dame la pata	Oh, Perica, give me your foot,
para ponerte las alpargatas.	so I may put on your sandals.

Cuando la perica quiere	When Perica wishes
que el perico coma arroz,	her husband to eat rice,
le salcocha la comida	she parboils the meal
y se la comen los dos.	and they both eat it.

Refrain: Ay, mi perica, . . .

Cuando la perica quiere	When Perica wishes
que el perico se enamore,	her husband to love her,
se quita las plumas viejas	she takes off her old feathers
y se viste de colores.	and dresses in bright colors.

Perica

Trans. by Olcutt Sanders   Chilean Folk Song

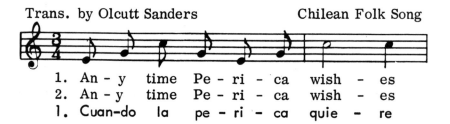

that her hus - band go to meet - ing,
that her hus - band eat his din - ner,
que el pe - ri - co va - ya_a mi - sa,

she a - ris - es Sun - day ear - ly,
she knows how he likes it par - boiled;
Se le - van - ta bien tem - pra - no

irons his shirts with fan - cy pleat - ing.
nei - ther of the two grows thin - ner.
y le plan - cha la ca - mi - sa.

Oh, my Pe - ri - ca, hold your foot
Ay, mi pe - ri - ca, da - me la

stead - y. I'll tie your san - dals;
pa - ta pa - ra po - ner - te

then you'll be read - y. read - y.
las al - par - ga - tas. ga - tas.

From *Amigos Cantando,* Cooperative Recreation Service, Delaware, Ohio, page 5. Permission to reprint granted by the publishers.

A LAS PUERTAS DEL CIELO
(At the Doors of Heaven)

A las puertas del cielo	At the doors of Heaven
venden zapatos	they sell shoes
para los angelitos	for the little angels
que están descalzos.	who are barefoot.

Refrain:

Duérmete, niño,	Sleep, child,
duérmete, niño,	sleep, child,
duérmete, niño,	sleep, child,
do-do, do-do, do-do,	. . .
Ave María, do-do.	

A los niños que duermen	The children who sleep,
Dios bendice,	God will bless.
a las madres que velan	The mothers who watch over
Dios las asiste.	them
	God will attend.

Refrain

From *Spanish Folk Songs of the Southwest,* collected and transcribed by Mary R. Van Stone, Academy Guild Press, Fresno, California. Permission to reprint granted by the publishers.

A las puertas del cielo
A Lullaby

Andantino

A las puer - tas del   cie - lo | ven-den za-pa-tos
At the   doors   of heaven | they sell shoes

pa - ra los an - ge - li - tos   que es - tán des - cal - zos.
for   little   angels   who   are   barefoot.

Duér - me - te, ni - ño,   duér - me - te, ni - ño,
Sleep my   child,   sleep   my child,

duér - me - te, ni - ño,   do - do,   do - do,
sleep,   my   child.

do - do,   A - ve Ma - rí - a, do - do.
Hail,   Mary.

EL TORTILLERO

(The Tortilla Vender)

Noche oscura, nada veo;	Dark night, I see nothing,
pero llevo mi farol.	But I carry my lantern.
Por tus puertas voy pasando,	I am passing by your doors
y cantando con amor.	and singing with love.

Refrain:

Mas, voy cantando	But I am singing
con harta pena.	with great pain.
¿Quién compra mis tortillas?	Who will buy my tortillas?
¡Tortillas buenas!	Good tortillas!

Bella ingrata, no respondes	Ungrateful, you do not reply
a mi grito placentero.	to my begging cry.
Cuando pasa por tu casa	When the tortilla vender
pregonando el tortillero.	shouts his wares by your house.

(Refrain)

Ya me voy a retirar con	Now I will leave with
mi canasta y farol,	my basket and lantern,
sin tener tu compasión	without your taking pity
de este pobre tortillero.	on this poor tortilla vender.

(Refrain)

From *Amigos Cantando*, Cooperative Recreation Service, Delaware, Ohio, page 24. Permission to reprint granted by the publishers.

The Tortilla Vender
El tortillero

Trans. by Olcutt Sanders

Chilean Folk Song

Thru the   dark-ness   now   I   wan-der
No-che o-scu - ra,   na - da   ve-o ;

with a lan-tern for my light. _____
pe-ro lle-vo mi fa-rol. _____

_____ Past your door-way I am go-ing;
_____ Por tus puer-tas voy pa-san-do,

So I'll sing a fond good-night. _____
y can-tan-do con a-mor. _____

Refrain:

Now _____ with deep sad-ness, _____
Mas, _____ voy can-tan-do _____

my _____ wares I cry them. ___ Who'll
con _____ har-ta pe-na. _____ ¿Quién

buy my good___ to-sta-di - tas? _____
com-pra mis ___ to-sta-di - tas? _____

1.
Tor - ti-llas! Buy them!
Tor - ti - llas bue - nas?

2.
Buy them!
bue - nas?

RIQUI RAN

Aserrín, aserrán,	Aserrin, aserran,
los maderos de San Juan	all the woodsmen of San Juan
comen queso, comen pan;	eat cheese and bread;
los de Rique, alfeñique;	those from Rique, sugar candy,
los de Roque, alfondoque,	those from Roque, loaf sugar,
ri-qui, ri-que, ri-qui, ran.	ri-qui, ri-que, ri-qui, ran.
Aserrín, aserrán,	Aserrin, aserran,
las abejas vienen, van;	the bees come and go;
miel laboran para el pan,	gather honey for their bread,
liban flores las de Rique,	those from Rique sip flowers,
cual almíbar de alfeñique,	like nectar of sugar candy,
y el panal de las de Roque	and the honey combs of Roque
se parece a un alfondoque,	are like a piece of loaf sugar,
ri-qui, ri-que, ri-qui, ran.	ri-qui, etc. . . .
Aserrín aserrán,	Aserrin, aserran,
los chiquillos, ¿dónde están?	where are all the children?
Todos a dormir se van.	All have gone to sleep,
Soñarán con alfeñique	to dream of white sugar candy
como sueñan los de Rique,	like those of Rique,
y mañana un alfondoque	and tomorrow a loaf sugar,
comerán con los de Roque,	they will eat with those from
ri-qui, ri-que, ri-qui, ran.	Roque,
	ri-qui, etc. . . .

From *Amigos Cantado,* Cooperative Recreation Service, Delaware, Ohio, page 13. Permission to reprint granted by the publishers.

Riqui Ran

Trans. by Olcutt Sanders

Latin-American Folk Song

A-se - rrín,   a - se - rrán,   all   the
A-se - rrín,   a - se - rrán,   los   ma -

woods-men   of   San   Juan   eat   their
de - ros   de   San   Juan   co - men

cheese and eat their   pan;   those from Ri-que, al-fe-
que - so, co - men   pan.   Los de   Ri-que al-fe-

ñi - que; those from Ro - que,   al - fon -
ñi - que; los   de   Ro - que,   al - fon -

*

do - que,   ri - qui,   ri - que, ri - qui   ran.
do - que,   ri - qui,   ri - que, ri - qui   ran.

MI CHACRA

(My Farm)

Vengan a ver mi chacra,	Come and see my farm,
que es hermosa.	for it is lovely.
Vengan a ver mi chacra,	
que es hermosa.	
El pollito hace así:	The chick goes this way:
ki-ki-ri.	
El pollito hace así:	
ki-ki-ri.	
O pas, camarade,	(French: "Walk in step,"
O pas, camarade,	pronounced: O pah,
o pas, o pas, o pas;	cah-mah-rahd.)
o pas, camarade, o pas camarade,	
o pas, o pas, o pas.	

My Farm

Mi chacra

Trans. by Olcutt and Phyllis Sanders   Argentine Folk Song

Quickly

Come, come and see my farm for it   is love-ly.
Ven - gan a ver mi cha-cra que_es her - mo-sa.

Come, come and see my farm for it   is love - ly.
Ven - gan a ver mi cha-cra que_es her-mo-sa.

Spoken

El po-lli-to goes like this: kee-kee-ree; el po-
El po-lli-to ha - ce_a-sí: ki - ki - ri; el po -

Spoken

lli- to goes like this: kee-kee-ree. O pas, ca-ma-rade,
lli-to ha - ce_a-sí: ki - ki - ri.

o pas, ca-ma-rade, o pas, o pas, o pas; o

pas, ca-ma-rade, o pas, ca-ma-rade, o pas, o pas, o pas.

QUE LLUEVA

Que llueva; que llueva,
La vieja de la cueva.
Los pajaritos cantan,
La madre se levanta.
Que sí, que no, ¡que llueva un chaparrón!
Agua, San Marcos, rey de los charcos,
Para mi triguito que está muy bonito;
Para mi cebada que está granada;
Para mi melón que ya tiene flor;
Para mi sandía que ya está florida;
Para mi aceituna que ya tiene una.

From a sampler of 32 songs. Used by permission of Cooperative Recreation Service, Inc., Delaware, Ohio.

Que llueva

Moderato ♩ = 108   Montevideo, Uruguay

It's rain-ing, it's rain-ing, old la-dy of the cave.
Que llue - va; que llue - va, la vie-ja de la cue-va.

The lit - tle birds are sing-ing, the moth-er's gone a-
Los pa - ja - ri -tos can - tan, la ma-dre se le -

Fine

wing-ing. Oh, yes, oh, no, the storm-y wind does blow!
van - ta. Que sí, que no, ¡ que llue-va un cha-pa-rrón!

Wa - ters, St. Mar-cus, king of the char-cos,
A - gua, San Mar- cos, rey de los char - cos,

After 5 repeats, D.C. al Fine

Para mi triguito que está muy bonito;
For my little wheatfield with beautiful rich yield;

Para mi cebada que está granada;
For my crop of barley, it's ripene'd so early;

Para mi melón que ya tiene flor;
Makes my melons grow with flowr's in a row;—

Para mi sandía que ya está florida;
Watermelons red—their vines blossom'd spread;

Para mi aceituna que ya tiene una.
For my olive tree—with olives for me.

LOS MAIZALES

(The Cornfields)

Song

1. *Los maizales brotan con primor,*
   fulguran sus hojas de color,
   el sol besó, su bello grano germinó.
   Tierra peruana de honor te embriagas.

2. *Después de la faena intelectual*
   Vamos presurosos a jugar,
   Cual nuestros padres al son del pan
   Vamos al campo a cultivar
   Tierra peruana de honor te embriagas.

Huayano Dance   A traditional dance of Peru.

The song tells of the flourishing cornfields, with their shining bright leaves, growing in the earth kissed by the sun. The second stanza says that, after working with our brains, let us hurry to the fields to grow our bread as our fathers did. The refrain is "Oh, Peruvian earth, you will be full of honor!"

1. Partners stand a few feet apart. With skipping step, (clicking heels) come together, bow and return to place.
2. Come together and circle around (back to back) and return to place.
3. Come together, hook right arms, circle, and back to place.
4. Take out handkerchiefs (girls hold handkerchief over head, boys hold handkerchief behind their backs).
   a. Come together, touching handkerchiefs, and return to place.
   b. Partners come together, hook handkerchiefs and turn in place to right, then to left, release handkerchiefs, and return to place.
5. Partners come together, boy places handkerchief around girl's neck and draws her forward as dance ends.

The dance step is a running hop step, with heels clicking. Clapping of hands during the dance is optional.

Los maizales

From *Hi Neighbor*. Book 6. U.S. Committee for UNICEF, Hastings House, publishers, New York. Permission to reprint granted by publisher.

TECOLOTE

(The owl)

Tecolote, ¿dónde viene?	Where do you come from owl?
Tecolote, ¿dónde viene?	
Yo vengo de Colorado,	I come from Colorado . . .
yo vengo de Colorado.	
Ay. Cu-cu-rru, cu, cu, cu,	
cu-cu-rru, cu, cu, cu,	
pobrecito animalito	poor little animal
tiene hambre,	is hungry, little owl. Oh.
Tecolotito, ay.	
Vengo a traerte una noticia,	I bring you news . . .
vengo a traerte una noticia,	
que tu amor ya es perdido,	That your love is lost . . .
que tu amor ya es perdido.	
Ay. Cu-cu-rru, cu, cu, cu,	
cu-cu-rru, cu, cu, cu,	
pobrecito animalito	
tiene hambre,	
Tecolotito, ay.	

Tecolote

¿dón - de vie - ne? Te - co - lo - te, ¿dón- de vie - ne?
un - a no -ti - cia, ven-go a traerte un-a no-ti- cia,

Yo   ven-go de   Co-lo-ra- do, yo   ven-go de
que   tu a-mor ya es per-di-do, que   tu a-mor

Co-lo-ra - do. Ay. Cu-cur-ru cu,   cu,
ya es per-di- do. Ay. Cu-cur-ru cu,   cu,

cu, cu-cur-ru, cu, cu,   cu,   po-bre-ci - to

an-i - mal-i-to t'ie-ne ham-bre, Te-co-lo-ti - to,   ay.

From *Spanish Folk Songs of the Southwest,* collected and transcribed by Mary R. Van Stone, Academy Guild Press, Fresno, California. Permission to reprint granted by the publishers.

NTC SPANISH TEXTS AND MATERIALS

Computer Software
Basic Vocabulary Builder on Computer
Amigo: Vocabulary Software

**Videocassette, Activity Book,
 and Instructor's Manual**
VideoPasaporte Español

Graded Readers
Diálogos simpáticos
Cuentitos simpáticos
Cuentos simpáticos
Beginner's Spanish Reader
Easy Spanish Reader

Workbooks
Así escribimos
Ya escribimos
¡A escribir!
Composiciones ilustradas
Spanish Verb Drills

Exploratory Language Books
Spanish for Beginners
Let's Learn Spanish Picture Dictionary
Spanish Picture Dictionary
Getting Started in Spanish
Just Enough Spanish

Conversation Books
¡Empecemos a charlar!
Basic Spanish Conversation
Everyday Conversations in Spanish

Manual and Audiocassette
How to Pronounce Spanish Correctly

**Text and Audiocassette Learning
 Packages**
Just Listen 'n Learn Spanish
Just Listen 'n Learn Spanish Plus
Practice and Improve Your Spanish
Practice and Improve Your Spanish
 Plus

High-Interest Readers
Sr. Pepino Series
  La momia desaparece
  La casa embrujada
  El secuestro

Journeys to Adventure Series
  Un verano misterioso
  La herencia
  El ojo de agua
  El enredo
  El jaguar curioso

Humor in Spanish and English
Spanish à la Cartoon

Puzzle and Word Game Books
Easy Spanish Crossword Puzzles
Easy Spanish Word Games & Puzzles
Easy Spanish Vocabulary Puzzles

Transparencies
Everyday Situations in Spanish

Black-line Masters
Spanish Verbs and Vocabulary Bingo Games
Spanish Crossword Puzzles
Spanish Culture Puzzles
Spanish Word Games
Spanish Vocabulary Puzzles

Handbooks and Reference Books
Complete Handbook of Spanish Verbs
Spanish Verbs and Essentials of Grammar
Nice 'n Easy Spanish Grammar
Tratado de ortografía razonada
Redacte mejor comercialmente
Guide to Correspondence in Spanish
Guide to Spanish Idioms

Dictionaries
Vox Modern Spanish and English Dictionary
Vox New College Spanish and English Dictionary
Vox Compact Spanish and English Dictionary
Vox Everyday Spanish and English Dictionary
Vox Traveler's Spanish and English Dictionary
Vox Super-Mini Spanish and English Dictionary
Cervantes-Walls Spanish and English Dictionary

For further information or a current catalog, write:
National Textbook Company
a division of *NTC Publishing Group*
4255 West Touhy Avenue
Lincolnwood, Illinois 60646-1975 U.S.A.